ABC Bo
Buying and Selling
Real Estate

The ABC Book of Home Buying

Thaddeus Faulknor

ABC Book of Buying and Selling Real Estate

The ABC Book of Home Buying

Published in the United States of America

ISBN 978-1-963379-99-0 (SC)
ISBN 978-1-963379-19-8 (HC)
ISBN 978-1-963379-20-4 (Ebook)

Library of Congress Control Number: 2024922814

Thaddeus Faulknor
222 West 6th Street
Suite 400, San Pedro, CA, 90731
www.stellarliterary.com

Ordering Information and Rights Permission:

Quantity sales. Special discounts might be available on quantity purchases by corporations, associations, and others. For details, contact the publisher at the address above.

For Book Rights Adaptation and other Rights Permission. Call us at toll-free 1-888-945-8513 or send us an email at admin@stellarliterary.com.

The ABC Book of Buying And Selling Real Estate

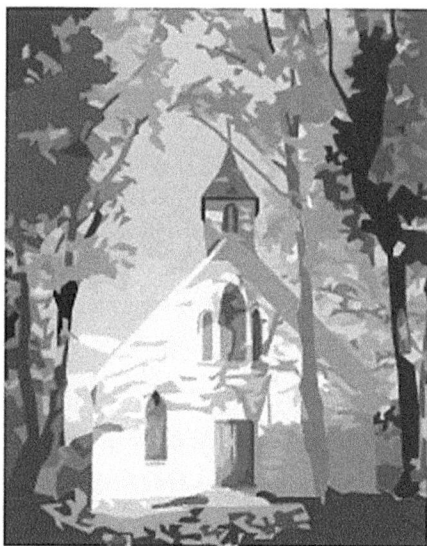

The ABC Book of Home Buying
BY: Thaddeus Faulknor

How to purchase your first home with
Little or no money down…

Buying Your First Home

Facts about your real estate transactions

PRINTED BY: Thaddeus Faulknor

Contents

Introduction...ix

Good Intentions.. 1

Buying Your First Home 5

A Good Realtor 16

What Price Home Can I Afford 19

Viewing Homes..21

How Many Houses Should I Look At Before Buying 25

Things You Should Look For When Buying A Home 28

Spotting Defects...30

House Hunting Tips 32

The Decision-Making Process 34

Should I Buy Or Rent 37

What Is An Equity?...45

Buying A New Home 47

Making Your Offer..51

Accepting Your Offer..54

Buyers Guide 57

Increase Your Property Value..59

Increase Your Credit Score 61

Home Owners Tips 64

The Basics Making An Offer 65

Why Do I Need An At Torney 67

Earnest Money Deposit...69

What Is A Home? 73

Finding A Bargain 76

When To Buy A Home 79

About Your Home...84

Hints On Calculating Your Mortgage 86

Buying A Foreclosure Home 105

How To Purchase With Little Or No Money 108

Should I Buy A Handyman Special? 111

How Do I Find Foreclosures 113

Establishing A Working Relationship 116

How Do I Sell My Home 119

Something That Will Make Your Home Sell 122

The Best Time To Sell 126

Marketing Your Home...128

What If My House Don't Sell 130

How Do I Price My House? 132

What Is A Fair Market Value? 134

Should I Fix My House Before I Sell It? 136

What Will Make My House Sell 139

Reaching Prospective Buyers 141

Showing Your House To Prospective Buyer 143

When Do I Start Looking For A Home? 146

Do I Need A Lawyer When Purchasing A Home? 148

How Do I Find The Best Bargain? 150

Real Estate And People 156

Real Estate And The Community 158

Caption Pages 160

Acknowledgements 162

INTRODUCTION

I was propelled to put out this little hand book because of the latest trend that the Real Estate Industry has taken. When you listen closely, you will hear more and more Americans complaining about the real estate market. Most people are very much concerned about the escalation of prices, and how inflation is eating up their income which makes it hard to own a home. In other words, the rapidly accelerating change has dampened their hopes of ownership. Many have to resort to taking two jobs to keep up with the times.

It can be seen clearly that the economy will not get better, and the financial challenges facing us will not get better but worse. Many times, we might have questions about our future, and try to find out what is ahead. There might not be any immediate solution to the questions and the crises which present themselves, but the beat goes on. These situations pose hard and tough decisions in these days and times. This is no fairy tale because many of us have listened to our friends and relatives complaining about this. The message that has been conveyed is quite plain and simple. Everything is at a fast rate of speed and has been eating up by inflation, therefore, simple logics will tell anyone to find a vehicle that accelerates faster than what we are experiencing. At the present time, we bow our heads over the classified ads section of the newspaper day after day with our markers in hand with their bright tips, confused and fed up, oh yes, but this will not solve the race to poverty.

In the pages that follow, you will come face to face with reality and realize that two jobs are not the real solution. I am not trying to frighten you, but we have got to learn how, and when to face the realities of life. I am trying to encourage you to learn to fish and not to settle for a one night of fish eating. This will only satisfy the immediate gratification and would not consider the days ahead. I want to share my knowledge with you; I want to help to begin a journey towards financial independence and self-reliance that will bring you the means for a promising future. I will borrow the words of the great Martin Luther King when he said" I have seen the promise land, and I know that one day I shall reach there, I know not when but mine eyes have seen it" Every one of us has faced with guns or butter decisions each day. Money spent is money earned; remember it takes money invested in real estate to bring all that butter. If you want to get ahead of inflation, I urge you to use the real estate edge which will accelerate faster and will give you the edge over the rate of inflation to catch up. The best vehicle to help catch up with inflation is real estate. You might not be sure of the type of real estate to go into, or when to do it, you may not have any prior knowledge, so that is why I am doing this book for you. I am not trying to take a bite out of your pocket, but show you how to add some resources to your portfolio. We called it dollars & cents. I am confident that real estate is for you.

If I may, I would like to introduce myself to my readers. To some, it might be interesting and to others not. Some of you reading my transcript might have known me personally, but whatever is your knowledge of me, the better it is for you to read what I have to say. There are many good things about the thoughts I have shared in this little hand book. I am confident that after reading this book you will not be as you were but will be ready to assume the challenges that lie ahead.

I have been to institutions of learning but my greatest teacher was the things that I have to do in order to share my knowledge with those of you that will seek to make strides, in search of excellence. In one of the epistles of Paul he penned these words. "From my youth, I have learned to know the Holy Scriptures," he went on to say, "It has made me wise unto salvation". My point is, from a youth, I have learned to like real estate and I would like to shed some light to someone desirous of getting in the real estate industry.

My road to real estate was by way of the wood work industry. After leaving high school, I thought it would be a good idea to learn carpentry and cabinet making. Why would I want to be a carpenter and a cabinet maker? One of the things I thought about was that I would build my home and later would be able to furnish it. Consequently, I embarked upon my thoughts and was able to show my experience in this fashion.

It was after visiting many different countries that I began working as a carpenter and cabinet maker. I then returned to my native Island of Jamaica where I taught the trade in high school for about six years. I then migrated to the United States, where I went to a higher institution of learning, but, amidst it all, I loved real estate and would not take anything for granted. Real estate for me can be the answer to my dreams, but I do not believe in just dreams, I believe that if a dream is to be lived, it has to become a reality. When we speak of real estate, what are we talking about? Real estate is to stop dreaming and to bring these dreams to reality. You are paying rent and dreaming of owning your home, but you have to stop talking about what you want to do and do it. Unless a significant step is taken, there will not be a completion. My real estate ambitions are not yet fully met, but I am on my way. No turning back. I believe that life owes every man a living, and it is for us to go in search of that which the Lord has in store for us. I am a strong believer in destiny.

GOOD INTENTIONS

I hope this little hand book will be helpful to everyone, (1) the Tenant (2) buyers, (3) sellers, and (4) investors. It was written specifically for those who want to learn more about the real estate industry without the knowledge of how or where to start. Some are even in but are afraid, of taking further steps. They are so afraid; they stay on safe grounds by doing nothing. My book addresses buyers and sellers alike. If you are buying for the first time or if you are a second time buyer, I can't stress enough to reminder you that each transaction is different and may have different levels of involvement.

It has been the American dream to buy real estate, nothing is wrong with that if it is a dream, but that dream should be fulfilled no matter what it takes. Sometimes the process of owning is hard and painful, but no one has promised an easy path to progress, therefore we should have the courage to weather the storm. I have spoken to several people on different occasions, including sellers, buyers, while others are undecided. However, whether or not you should enter the real estate arena or just remain a tenant, there is nothing to risk.

I would like to enlighten the minds of the buyers and sellers alike. I have walked the streets on many occasions and have listened to many people over the years. Most have done some real estate transactions while others have not. As an experienced real estate person, I would like to help both sellers and buyers alike, even those that have not yet decided what they want to do. There are three categories of people, and I am directing my thoughts to all three, the first are the ones that are still young in the business and still need plenty of guidance. The second is looking for a home and is just waiting for the opportunity to get in, and the third will never think of ownership.

This book will help you to see your needs, and more so identify those needs. I do however have concerns sometimes for the new buyer. They are new to the industry and are not quite sure of the first step to take. 2Most times they do not know the first question to ask. I would like to give some inside tips on the process of buying and selling. To those that are on the edge, I would like to say this effectively, and try to educate my readers. If I could only enlighten the minds of my readers, my goals would have been met.

We are well aware that the task of buying a home is not an easy one; therefore, one has to be strong along with great determination. It is a big step that has to be well thought of and should be entered in to very thoughtfully. A well-informed buyer is what I like to see. A well-informed buyer he or she will get a better result. If I could explain and outline this effectively, the object of this book would have been met. This is why I took on to myself the pain of writing so this message could be conveyed through this book. I realized that I cannot be everywhere to meet with everyone, but as you read on, you will find this to be an article of dedication and of concern for those wanting to enter the real estate industry not only to buy one parcel, but to make a honest living in an honest and ethical manner. This is more than a pep talk, because after talking, you will forget most of what was said, with this book you will have it handy when the information is needed.

I would like this book to help you become financially independent. This can only happen if you read the book and apply yourselves accordingly. Many of you have worked very hard over the years and have not owned a piece of Real Estate. This does not have to be so, but you have to be willing and able to risk something, and that something is money. Time equals more money and this is what we are talking about when we refer to financial independence. I would suggest that after you read this book, if at all you find it helpful, tell someone about it or better yet, give it to someone you know as a gift, and you will be glad you did. They will appreciate such a gift. You know we would like to go about and feed all our friends and enemies with fish because they like to eat fish, but since it is so hard, we teach them how to catch fish so they can feed themselves and their loved ones for life. What a great thing to do, if only you could help somebody, why not help them? This book was not meant to teach a course in real estate. However, it is essential that you learn about the real estate industry, and as a real estate broker, I definitely have a working knowledge of the market. I understand how it should be entered in and, I want to share these skills with you. I want you to obtain the best possible deal when attempting to buy real estate. .

Keep in mind that good knowledge will not make a bad deal good. It is only the knowledge used to put the deal together that makes it work. You must examine the kind of deal and determine whether it fits the type of investment you are considering to get into or to add to your portfolio. Good knowledge will keep a good deal intact and may eliminate many potential conflicts between buyers and sellers alike.

Please note that this booklet will act as a pioneering effort, due to the interpretation of many of the provisions that have been tested in any situation. The material in this explanatory manual is for illustration purposes, the only purpose of this material is to explain some of the knowledge gathered in the real estate industry and to provide an illustration of how to purchase a home wisely. Note however, that all transactions are different and should be treated differently. Like a good suit of clothes each should be tailored to a good fit and will fit differently.

BUYING YOUR FIRST HOME

B uying your first home is a major step and should be entered in carefully.

I have tried to compile these ideas in a comprehensive manner that deals with the sellers and buyers a like. I will deal with the buying and later take you to the selling aspect of the real estate market. A buyer is one that is in the market to purchase a piece of real estate; notice I did not use the words "first time". First time buyers are those that are living in a rental property or living with someone, but do not own a property for themselves. By the way, if you sold your property and did not own for three years, and are now looking to purchase after the three years, you are now considered a first-time buyer. You are permitted to actively engage in the market as first-time homebuyers. It does not matter what you are looking to purchase, it could be a co-op, condo, or a one to three family home that you are going to live in.

Now that you are a potential home buyer, don't get too anxious, you might want to know why shopping for your home takes a lot more than just looking at houses. This is why it is in your best interest to have a qualified Realtor with adequate knowledge and skill to provide you with the service you need. You have worked tirelessly for your money, some of you put forty or more hours per week to make regular savings, therefore, you want to know that you are doing the right thing. That is why you should not get too anxious, or else you could get into the wrong home or may even lose your money. Remember, do not get too anxious, I cannot emphasize this enough, you will agree with me later. I think money is hard to accumulate so we should spend it wisely. Honest money comes one way, but there are several ways for it to leave our hands, therefore, we should make good use of it when it is in our possession, don't you agree?

Now that you are looking forward to the day when you shall own a piece of the American dream, and fulfill your desires, I urge you not to let your dreams turn into a nightmare and go down the tubes. Your goals should be closely followed until they are fulfilled. Nothing is wrong with dreaming of becoming a home owner, but you should seek the help of a Realtor. You may ask, why do you have to consult a realtor when you could do it by yourself? Sure, you could go and do your home shopping, but since you are new to the market you may overlook some very important points and things you should know. There are things you may never know until it's too late. I recall a few years ago a seller called me up and said, "I want you to sell my home ". I made an appointment for the next day. When I got to the home, the seller said, "Look through and tell me how much I could get for my home" I looked and told him that he could put the home on the market for $220,000. He rejected my price and said he wanted $260,000 I could not sell the property for $260,000; it was not worth the price he wanted. His response to me was, "If the broker can't get my price, I will get it from someone off the street, so I will sell it myself and get my price. "Very true", I replied, because they will pay over the price. In a matter of two weeks the seller called me. I thought he was telling me to sell his home, instead, he said to me that "you did not sell my home but I got it sold and I got the price I wanted". I asked him, "who bought the home?" His reply was, "Someone walked off the street". "Good luck", I replied. About one month later the same seller called again and informed me that his home was back on the market and he wanted me to help him find a buyer. I asked, "What happened to the buyer you had"? His reply was "The lady could not come up with the money to complete the transaction, so she lost the deal and the down payment of $10,000". If the purchaser had used a real estate agent, she would not have lost her deposit. For first time home buyers, you cannot be too careful. Remember you have worked five to ten years to accumulate your money, so you are able to purchase a place to call home, don't treat it lightly.

There are a few tips that I would like to share with you before you get fully involved in the buying process. This is very important, because it will take approximately five to ten years of savings to purchase your first home, therefore you should be careful entering this process. Getting a professional to help will not hurt you but will help you. Even if it costs you a couple of dollars, it will be worth every penny when it is all over. You can trust me on this one; I have personal experience in this area.

As an owner and realtor, I have seen the need for this straight talk with you prospective first-time homebuyers. You will one day be proud homeowners, but don't get too overwhelmed in the process. I know what the feeling is. I have been there before you. It's there, but don't let it get ahead of you. Do not let the dream of having your backyard for barbequing on Independence Day get to you. Your dreams could be shattered even before they are materialized. I have seen potential buyers looking for homes, and even before they found it, they have their moving date. This is not a good way for shopping for a home; you are putting too much pressure on yourself. In this way, you may settle for something that you could do better on. Looking in a hurry because you want a back yard for Independence Day is not a good enough reason to go shopping for a home in a rush. I remember a potential buyer came to me and wanted to find a home the next day, I tried to slow him down to take the pressure off himself. I could not help him because he was moving a little too fast and not until I stopped him before I could give a better sense of direction. He claimed that I was not working along with him. Real estate is not a purchase in a rush. It is your money, you have worked hard for it, so don't be in a rush to get rid of it. It is going to take you a long and hard effort to replenish those funds. When you are ready to start shopping, talk to realtor first. You have heard, "have patience" all your life and guess what? I am going to tell you the same thing; you must be patient when you are shopping for a property. The worst thing you could do is to purchase impulsively, and then lose your money. This can and will happen. There are a few things that should be taken care of before you start looking at properties and are influenced by the overwhelming spirit that lights your face. You need to make sure you can obtain a mortgage if you are not buying for cash. A lady came to me some time ago and told me that she wanted to purchase a co-op, I asked her if she was purchasing for cash, she asked me "what do I mean for cash"? Cash means that you have all the money that is needed to complete the transaction without going to the bank for a loan. If the home you are looking to purchase costs ($150,000), and you already have $160,000 in your bank account, that is your money with no strings attached. You have worked for that money and you have made continuous savings each time you get your paycheck, or someone may have given you a gift or maybe you were a lucky winner in a lottery draw. If any of these is the case, and you have enough money to complete the sales transaction, it is considered a cash deal. If this is the case you would not have to go to a bank to negotiate a loan.

Buying your first home is not an easy task. It is one of the most challenging procedures that you may ever have in your life. It comes with great pride and experience, and the end result is very rewarding and overwhelming, although others may see it as frustrating. A well-trained real estate agent with good knowledge and skill will always have that silver touch to bring the transaction through smoothly. He or she has a wealth of information at their fingertips, and many more at their disposal. They know where to get the necessary information. This will also give you some buying power, if or when a person sees a cash buyer. The negotiation process becomes easier than when someone has to go to the bank for a mortgage, why? because, the deal can close in a much faster time than going to a lending institution. Cash deals can close within weeks compared to a sale that is going through a bank which could take months, as much as 2-3 months, and depending on which state you are in it which could take more time if difficulties arise.

Now, let's say that you are going to the bank for a mortgage; they would have to do your credit check to see if there are credit issues. If there are no credit problems, the bank or your mortgage officer would get you a pre-qualification letter. This letter would state your possibilities in obtaining your mortgage. Based upon your credit report, it will determine the type of interest rate the bank will give to you. Banks are in the business of making money. They make their monies by lending it to people who are eligible for loans. Banks make most of their money by lending it to homeowners. Once your credit meets their criteria and you accept the bank's term of the loan, you are ready to go home shopping.

By the way, it is good to use a real estate broker, if you so desire. It doesn't matter where you live, you will hear about realtors, so choose one that's in your area. You can locate realtors by watching television programs, in the telephone directory, the radio, or you can purchase a newspaper. Don't be afraid to call for an appointment. Let them know you are in the process of buying your first home, and they will be glad to talk with you, and you will be glad you did too. Realtors are licensed by the state in which they work so as to conduct business in an ethical manner.

A good realtor is more than just a sales person, this you will find out when you start talking to one. They will help you to make some very good decisions. It is very important that you like your real estate agent because you will be working with him or her between 80-120 days. It could take you this much time before finding the home you are looking for. Meeting with your agent to discuss what your needs are, is a good idea which will put you in a comfort zone with your realtor.

By then you will know if you are comfortable with him or her. Realtors can be of great help to you in many ways. Try to find a realtor who is a member of a Multiple Listing Service in your area. They will show you more properties than you could find on your own. When you choose your agent, meet with him or her to discuss the kind of home you are looking for. It is important for you to discuss the location, the size, the style, the price and any other features or requirements you may need. This means that you and your agent will be together for a long time looking at houses which also may cause frustration, especially if you do not like the realtor.

Remember not to look at any property that is above your budget. Your agent will tell you what the price range is, so try to stay in that range. You could ask your realtor to show you homes that are available for sale, and you will see the price range and the location of these homes. If you want to shop by yourself, your local newspaper is an excellent source of finding homes that are for sale by owners. Driving and scouting out the neighborhood where you would like to live is another way of finding "for sale" homes. These homes are called "for sale by owners", (F.S.B.O). It is better to negotiate with F.S.B.O sometimes because there are no agents involved. Your chance of getting a better deal may increase.

There are important factors to consider when buying. This will be your home and you are planning to live there for many years. It is a place that you will have to raise your family. It doesn't matter how many times you go away; you will have to come back to your home. Make sure it has the closet space you need, or the space to build one if you have to do so later. What about parking for your car? It does not make sense to do your purchasing and the following day after moving in you are complaining about space to park the car. You should think about that before, think about the things that are necessary for the comfort of your home. These are some of what will make your home enjoyable and a comfortable place to live.

While taking these things into consideration, think about budget, the type and price of home you can afford. If you want all the convenience in a home then you would have to think of affordability. Affordability is simply, "Can I afford the things that I am going after? If you want everything in a home then you know that you would have to pay the price. On the other hand, if your taste is for a pricey home that you cannot afford, let me tell you that you are just fooling yourself. It would be good for you to listen to your realtor; because he or she might just be your reality check. A pricey home will, and can put you into serious trouble in a very short period of time. You have to remember that it is not just a one- time thing, because you will have to face a monthly payment for thirty years. That is a very long time to have the monkey on your back; you just cannot get rid of it so easily unless you sell the home, or default on the mortgage, and the bank is going to start foreclosure proceedings on the property. I don't think you want that to happen to you, so that's the reason why I stress affordability. This is what I am guarding you against. If you cannot afford the home, you are looking at, leave it and move on to something else that you can really afford without stretching your budget. If you stretch it too thin it will get you into trouble.

Your income determines the value of the home that you can purchase. Don't be fooled; a sixty thousand income cannot purchase a five hundred-thousand-dollar home. If you are thinking of that, believe me you are not going to make it unless you are putting down a substantial amount of money when you are negotiating the contract. The other exception to the income rule is, if you can find a co-signer to co-sign for you. A co-signer is someone that is willing to put his income against yours so you could have a combined higher income to purchase a more expensive home. For example, your income is sixty thousand dollars and the other person's income is also sixty thousand. These two incomes are combined to give the purchasers more buying power. Remember, a co-signer could be anyone. They could be mother, father, brother, sister, or any other relative, or even a good friend. An interesting point to note is that the co-buyer does not have to live in the home with you. He or she is asking in good faith on your behalf to help you qualify for the mortgage. This is the reason why your agent should try to find out how much money you are working with, so if you need a co-signer, they would be able to give you the correct information before they waste their time, and you the buyer start building your hopes and later have it shattered all because they did not start out correctly. Trying to find out your gross income is just a matter of finding out if you would be qualified for the price home you are considering. Most times when Realtors try to help buyers by trying to find out the amount of money that they the customers are working with, they become defensive, and do not want to make such disclosure but that is just to assist you better. They are not going to take your money, of a true they will know how much money you have to put into the home you are about to purchase. Trust me, Realtors will not try to take your monies like that, they ask questions to help you the buyer make an intelligent decision and not to waste too much time. As you know, time is equal to money so, we try to save it as much as possible. When you spend a lot of time looking for a home that you cannot afford, you are wasting time and if you should do that a couple of days or weeks you are going to become very frustrated and disappointed not only that, but you are going to fire your Realtor. I do not want that to happen to you, so I am trying to prevent it. The monthly payment on your mortgage has to be affordable even when using a co-signer.

Could you imagine walking into a realtor's office and ask him or her for a two-family home, the agent takes you into his or her car around town until you find what you wanted then you make an offer. It was accepted, so you contacted your attorney who asked you to sign the contract with your deposit of ($25,000) twenty-five thousand dollars. You informed the attorney that "all you had was ($15,000) fifteen thousand dollars". What would you say? What would you do? You would have fired your agent because he did not do a good job for you. These are some of the reasons why we say you should talk to your real estate agent as they are well trained. They are your specialist and will make sure that you do not waste time, because they do not want to waste their time either. Their objective is to get you the home that you can afford in the shortest possible time, and have you close so you can move in and be settled. I will constantly remind you in this writing that buying a home is not an easy task. This is one reason why your realtor does not want to keep this dragging for a long time; therefore, you should cooperate with him and give it your best shot. Some buyers think they should be shown every home in the neighborhood before deciding on one. I had a couple who visited me once, looking for a home. They asked me to show them all the one family homes in the area for sale. I asked them why they wanted to see all one family homes when they wanted to purchase a two family, "Just to see what is out there", they replied. I want to inform you of the system we have in place, so that we do not go all over town trying to find the right home for you. By the time you finish reading this book you will understand more about what I am saying regarding the purchasing of a home.

To find the right property you might have to decide how much time you are willing to spend per day or per week looking at properties. There are some people that recommend two hour per day going through the neighborhood that might be of interest to you and your family. I know you have already had the area established in your mind, so when you are driving you are not really wasting your time. This is a good way of doing things on your own after enough asking around, and you are sure where you want to live.

A GOOD REALTOR

There are some things that you should know about a realtor before you choose one. Realtors are experienced and professional people, who are highly trained in the real estate industry to assist buyers and sellers alike, so don't be afraid of them. It is good to make friends with realtors; they want to do the same with you. You will need their professional advice as time progresses. Realtors are supposed to be honest and do things ethically. If you have a friendly realtor, he or she will always look out for your best interest in case something good comes up, and will be on your side. Many realtors do have a good knowledge of the real estate industry and they are willing to share their expertise and knowledge once they are put to the test.

Realtors are willing to give pertinent information regarding buying or selling real estate, don't refuse as this could be a legacy of power in your endeavor. They have gone through vigorous training and hard work to be where they are. Many have spent relentless hours attending seminars and various training in order to get reliable information to share with the public. They are proud of their results. Realtors do believe in the code of ethics, which is vital to the industry, and separates us from other businesses. This helps us to foster our cooperative efforts to exchange information with other Realtors.

Realtors are a registered collective membership and are members of the National Association of Realtors. We subscribe to its strict code of ethics. We do this because we like what we do best in the interest of our community and those we serve. A good realtor does not believe in a tarnished image, but work hard to be credible and trust worthy. We pledge to take all possible precautions   to discourage any attempts that would tarnish the image of our industry. Our aim is always to increase our professionalism so that we can be successful, and strive to represent our buyers and sellers with dignity. We encourage people of every group and background to join us in our endeavor to build a strong community and a reputable organization.

Most people have seen real estate as an opportunity for cashing in, therefore, we have to keep it looking good and attractive until the sun sets. We will continue to hold ourselves and our fellow associates worthy, dignified and credible in this wonderful resilient industry. Although we do take on certain risks, sometimes by working with buyers without a contract, this sometimes leaves us vulnerable to waste precious time without being compensated, yet we take that risk. We trust you the public to cooperate with us in our endeavor to strive in this lucrative industry to serve you better. It is through our skills and training that we have provided such professionalism to help you achieve the dream of your life time. It is our endeavor as realtors to serve you in the most professional way we can, and to provide you with professional assistance as much as possible. Realtors rely on the buyer's loyalty before investing time and energy into pursuing a home that meets the needs of the buyers.

Realtors have been helping people over the years to buy and sell their homes. We do know too well what an exciting yet uncertain time it can be. Time and repeated success bring about uncertain expectations. The real estate industry is one that the public has expected a lot from and as professionals, we promise responsiveness and integrity to our people. Not only that, but we promise commitment that will earn the trust of buyers and sellers alike. We do understand the responsibilities that come with making your home buying or selling a pleasure. We know that you the public are counting on us expecting our very best, and certainly we would not want it to be any other way. Upon these promises, we solicit your cooperation in what we do best.

WHAT PRICE HOME CAN I AFFORD

There is no one that can readily tell you as a buyer the price home that you can afford, unless they sit with you and find out some specifics, such as cash that is available to you, the length of time on the job etc. By talking to your agent, he or she will be able to give you a good sense of direction regarding the purchase of your new home. This is what a good and experienced agent will do for you. Although your agent is not the one giving you finances, they know the process, and will know financial institutions that they work with on a regular basis. They can refer you to someone they know. Your agent will know the price home that you can afford; of which I have stated earlier that the price is commensurate with your income. You must also have a legal source of income in order to secure a mortgage from a reputable lending institution.

We have found this to be a big problem in today's real estate market.

Many people would like to purchase a piece of property, wanting to secure some kind of financing on the property but do not have the resources needed to do so. There are potential purchasers that are looking to buy a home for $300,000 while their income is $40,000. They just cannot afford the property and at the same time fail to accept the fact that they cannot afford the property. To tell you the truth, 'you are just wasting your time and fooling yourself." The good thing is that you won't be able to fool your agent, if you do, shame on him, because he is the one to direct you in your search of becoming a homeowner. There are many buyers that do not know what it takes to purchase a home that is why I advise you not to sell yourself short, talk to a good agent. He is committed to hard work, service, and responsibility, dedication and determination. A good agent will work for his client and he will find all the available resources for you. He will help you to find something that will fit your budget. You may even be surprised at just how much you could afford. For more tips on mortgages and financing you can talk with a bank specialist, or if you do not know one ask your realtor to refer you to one. They know plenty of them. They will not hesitate in recommending a mortgage Company or a consultant. They are the ones with money so you have to talk with them although you might not want to hear what they have to say sometimes.

What a purchaser may be qualified for mortgage wise may not be what he/ she wants to pay as his/her monthly mortgage payment. The bank may qualify the purchaser for more than what they are willing to pay for on a monthly basis. This will also affect the determination in the price of a home. The monthly payment is commensurate with the mortgage amount. The down payment plus the closing equals the amount of money needed to close on the property.

VIEWING HOMES

Once you are pre-qualified by your financial institution, it is time to target homes in your price range and your desired location. When viewing homes, your realtor will show you homes that you would not normally see without an agent. These homes are listed with the (MLS.) Multiple Listing Service in your area. They can only be accessed by Realtors that are members of that organization. To make it easier, they can just enter the specific criteria of your home such like number of bedrooms, bathrooms, and square feet including price range and the computer will bring up all the homes within the category of the information that was entered by the Realtor. Normally this cannot be done by a non-participant of the Multiple Listing Service and that is why I urge you to ask your realtor if he or she is a member of the Board of Realtors. You will get better service as well as being able to view more homes in a much shorter period of time.

You might want to know what the benefits are of using such Realtors but it is simple. The realtor that has the access to the system will be able to show more homes in a shorter period of time. There would be more homes from which you could make your selection, so that means you would spend less time looking to find your dream home and the home of your choice. In this case, if your move is in a hurry your MLS Realtor would be the one to get you in and out of the home shopping area in the shortest possible of time. When you are shopping or viewing the home, ask all the questions that come to your mind. Sometimes your mind goes blank and it might seem that you run short of words or you may not have any questions until you reach home. I encourage you to have a pen and paper handy so you can make notes. As you remember something write it down, you cannot forget what is written, it is just a matter of reflection when you want to remember what your thoughts were and the questions you would like to ask. Don't be afraid, you are about to spend the earnings of your life so you need to be informed as much as possible. Every question is important to you. Ask about the schools in the neighborhood, the shopping, and take in consideration the business and on the street to see if that is where you want your children to be raised. What about a place of worship, is that important to you? If so, ask about the Churches in the area, the more informed you are the better it will be for you to make your decision.

These might be of importance to you when you move, therefore you should address them now rather than have the consequences of dealing with them. When viewing the home, do not look at the furniture, you are not buying furniture you are buying the home, unless you will be buying the furniture later on. If so, do not get confused with the home and the furniture, they are two separate transactions. When you are viewing a home, look on the floor to see if it is level or saggy. Look on the roof for possible defects. If you like the home and are going into a contract with the seller, it is time you hire an engineer to check the structure of the home. An engineer will see a lot more than you can ever imagine. This is their area of work and they will do a good job for you. The cost of about ($500) five hundred dollars for a engineer inspection could save you a lot of money and also some headaches later after you have moved into the home. He will check the roof, the floor, plumbing and electrical systems, the boiler, the walls etc. There might be other things that are needed to be looked into. Therefore, you will get your money's worth.

I remind you not to look on carpet and painting; those are really cosmetics that can be done at minimal cost. Spotting defects sometimes can be hard, but I want you to be happy after you have moved in, so I encourage you to do it sooner rather than dealing with it later. I do not want you to discover two weeks later that your home has termites or the floor is lean, all these could have been easily avoided only if you had done the right thing by seeking the help of an expert. A major structural or mechanical system or problem in a home can derail a smooth purchase. A competent home inspector can protect you from getting caught by a significant defect after you have moved in. Although sellers are required to disclose any major problems, they are aware of, you should try to detect some obvious defects yourself. You are to keep in mind things like a bad roof. Look for marks on ceilings which are very serious problem and can be very costly to be corrected. You can make notes of the defects as you spot them on each property. This will help you as you move from one home to another, instead of trying to remember all of the defects you have seen on each home by memory. Don't just trust your memory it could fail you and you are going to use the word "I think I had seen level floors" now that you are seeing a sagging floor. If the floor has a defect put it down, "floor is saggy," or roof needs replacing, kitchen sink leaks. You see, when you get home you do not have to start to fall in a trance to remember what you saw, and on what property you saw it. When you make notations, put the address of property where you saw the problem. You will be surprised how helpful this kind of checklist will be to you.

HOW MANY HOUSES SHOULD I LOOK AT BEFORE BUYING

There is no such set of rules to say the number of houses should be looked on before deciding if an offer should be made. If you make a list of the features, you are looking for in your home such as: the number of bedrooms, whether you need dining or an eat-in kitchen; provide your agent with as much details as possible, so he or she can be precise in finding your home on your first visit. That is fine, and you will have less aggravation traveling all over to find a property of your choice. Not only that, but to drive looking on ten houses when you have already saw what you wanted does not make too much sense.

I remember looking for a home for a very large family, I sat with them for sometimes asking them several questions. I tried to find out the size of the family, how old the children were, and they were very much cooperative. Sometimes I asked certain questions and they asked why I was asking so many questions. I replied, "Because I want to be of help. They sometimes laugh; nevertheless, they answer my questions. I remember the father asking me, "When are you going to show us a house?" My reply was, I could not show you a property until I gather the relevant information. I wanted to show the right property, because the family was very large and I did not want to waste time. Two weeks later I made a call to the family, they were overjoyed. One of them asked "Have you found a house for us?" I hesitated but later answered "Yes", "When can we see the property, they asked?" "Today", I replied. A meeting was scheduled for the next day. The next day the family came down, I showed them the home, I was not in a hurry, I gave them all the time they needed to inspect the property. They walked to the back yard and it was ok. "We are ready now" one of them said to me. "We like the property and we do not want to see another; this is it; this is what we were looking for". "Bull's eye" I shouted; this was the first home I showed the family.

What happened was that I did my homework correctly. I spent some time with them, I tried to find out all what they were looking for, so that when I went out the first time, I would find the right property.

The first home may be awaiting you on your first trip, so who would say you should not take it? You might want to know more about the neighborhood. Stop by the Chamber of Commerce and pick up some promotional literature about the community. You do not have to make a decision right there, take them home, read them so you can make the right decision with the family, or whomever may be involved in the purchasing or the decision making. You could even visit some of the citizens in the area and make friends with them, tell them you are considering moving unto the area and listen to them carefully. When they talk with you, you may be glad you did. The information you get might encourage you to move in or tell you to go some other place. That is not the right place for you, whichever way it goes you will get some information that will be helpful to you and then you will not go wrong. While you are with the owners and have developed a rapport with them, don't forget to ask them for names of people they know who might be interested in selling. Tell them you will pay a $100 finder's fee to anyone that provides information leading you into contract. Nothing is wrong with that; I think they would be more willing and cooperative to help you finding a home. If you ask enough questions and the right ones, you will get all kinds of information. I think being able to talk to people is the most important ingredient to success in this whole program. Some people are really friendly, and you will meet some as you travel around town or the country.

THINGS YOU SHOULD LOOK FOR WHEN BUYING A HOME

If this is the first home you are looking to purchase there are some things that you may want to consider. Before you start shopping around, it would be helpful to you so start making some notes, you may not remember the things you should be looking for, but if you make a list, you would be able to take it with you and as you walk through the homes, you would have your check list to look through. So, don't be afraid, take your time and check your items one at a time and when you are through looking, you will find out that you are more satisfied, because you have done a more thorough job than if you had not made a list.

I like the checklist because there are so many things to look for when buying a home. You will never remember everything, so don't depend on your memory unless you have a computer in your brain. What will happen is that when you get home you will be asking yourself many questions such as: did I see a dishwasher, or was there an air conditioner in the bedroom? I remember going to show an apartment for sale. I was not the listing agent. The buyer looked at the apartment once, twice, and was satisfied, so she told me she would like to purchase the apartment. We went into contract and then to closing. At the closing, she asked for the air conditioning unit and I asked her which air conditioning unit she was referring to, her response was, the one in the living room. I explained to her there was no air conditioner. Her reply was, "I thought I saw an air conditioner and I would like to have it." This situation has occurred many times on different occasions and I do not want this happen to you.

As a prospective homeowner, you now have an idea of what you are looking for to call home for you and your family. Therefore, I cannot warn you more. I will agree that there are many things that you might not know, therefore, do not make a big issue of these things. For instance, if you are buying your first home, you do not really need a swimming pool so you do not make a big issue of it. A fireplace is nice, but do you really need a fireplace when you are just getting your first experience of home ownership? I would encourage you to forget those things that are not so important in your first home. I suggest you look for the basic things that are needed relevant to your everyday living.

For your protection, as a buyer that you try all the light switches. Turn on all faucets, and look out for the water pressure. Turn them on and off to make sure they are working. You should run the shower, flush the toilet, turn on the furnace and the air conditioning unit. By doing so, you will know from the get go if they are working. Although you will hire a professional later, everything that you can possible test should be tested. All deficiencies should be noted and your realtor should be informed, and later be forwarded to your Attorney who will make sure you are compensated to get the repairs done before you close, or else he might request the work be done before the closing of the property takes place.

SPOTTING DEFECTS

L ooking for defects can be very costly, and I would not want you to purchase your home and by the time you move in you are faced with a big repair bill that you cannot afford. This is why I am encouraging you to get an inspector to go through the home even before you make any kind of commitment. If you know what to look for, there might be some things that you could pick up on your first visit, and if that be the case you would save yourself sometime by not making a second trip to the home, and secondly, by not engaging an inspector to tell you what is wrong from what is not.

A major structural problem in a home can derail a smooth transaction. A competent home inspector can protect you from getting caught by a significant defect after you have made the offer. At the same time, I urge you to try and spot obvious defects yourself. When I speak of serious defects, I am talking about a sagging roof, the shingles might be blown off and water getting into the roof which could be very costly to you if detected after the purchase. Water stains can be an indication of leakages and should not be over looked although sometimes it is fixed but the water stain is still there, but you should ask about it. There is never be a cost to ask, but if you do not ask it can be costly to fix, therefore, I would ask because it is cheaper to ask than not to.

You have to remember though, you are not buying a new home so there will be repairs, but I would prefer if they are small repairs that will cost a couple of dollars and not anything to let you pull your hair out. Do not worry over things like a hole in the wall that is not expensive to repair, or a door falling off or cannot be locked, painting or a cracked tile that need to be changed. These things you will find into the home that are to be fixed. My word to you is, "do not worry about these small things" and do not let them derail a sale. They can be corrected easily and cheaply, but if you cannot handle them, and don't know what it takes to get these minor repairs done, the key to this is to get someone look at it before you even sign any papers. Here is what you do; ask your realtor to take you back to the home, he or she will make a date for you with the owner. Once you get the date and time to go to the home, ask someone you know who can do the work or ask someone that already own a home. It is possible that person knows someone that worked for him. When you get a hold of the person tell him that you will be closing on this home very soon, and you would like him to do some work once you close, therefore he should look on the work and give an estimate of the cost and you would have the money to pay him as soon as he finishes the work. What do you think? Would he go to look on the job and give you an estimate of the work? Sure, he will. Then you take him to the home with the broker and show him the work that needs to be done, right away you will know what the repairs are going to cost you, and there and then you could make an intelligent decision on the purchasing of the property. If you had made an offer, you could ask that the price, be adjusted based upon the price the workman gave you to fix the existing problems. If you did not make an offer now you can do so intelligently because you have the funds to do the repairs. You could take the repair cost from the offer you intended to submit.

HOUSE HUNTING TIPS

House hunting tips are when you have decided that this is the time for you to start looking around for the home you want to live in with your family. It is the place called home, possible where you might live for the rest of your life. By now you should have your pre- qualification letter from a bank which involves your job, meaning, your income, your credit worthiness, interest rate, the type of loan you have selected and how much ready cash you have available for your down payment and closing cost, among other factors that might have surfaced.

Closing cost is the money needed at the day of closing when you will be taking possession of the property. It is being used to pay several bills in your behalf at the time of closing. I had several people asking me times upon times, can I avoid paying closing cost? Do I have to pay it? What is it for? So now you do not have to be mistaken, you have to pay closing cost. Your closing cost and your down payment would be the total amount of money you need to have when purchasing your home. You don't have to guess or estimate the amount of money you need to buy a home or how much you can afford;

your mortgage broker will give you a full assessment of what you need. The letter your lender will give you qualifies you for a certain amount, that is the amount of home you will be able to purchase, money wise. This amount may surprise you as it may be less than what you were thinking, or it may be much more than you thought. Whatever the case, that will be the basis the realtor will use to show you a home.

An important point here is when you are going to view the property, everyone that will be involved in the decision making of the purchasing should go to the viewing. This will be a good move and will save potential argument in the future. You see, with all potential buyers, viewing the home and making the decisions, there is likely to be less argument regarding features that should be there or should not be there. All the visiting potential buyers will be conducting their own observation, in this way you will see more than what one person will have normally seen. This should be a joint effort and should be dealt with in a joint manner. When this is done, there won't be any finger pointing after the closing, neither any can one person can be blamed. This is a wonderful step that should be taken and completed wisely, joyfully and more so at the end, the Realtors and every one should be happy. Many buyers are overwhelmed upon the first visit to the Realtors office before the shopping process starts. Ask all the questions you can, this may be good. Voluntarily talk about what you have in mind as it could of importance. It does not matter who you are, you have to learn to take action and do the things you want to do. You determine the action to get accomplishment. There is no other time than now. This could just be the beginning of your real estate education. Realtors do not consider any question foolish only educational. If you do not ask them, we will not ask them for you and we will think that you already know.

THE DECISION-MAKING PROCESS

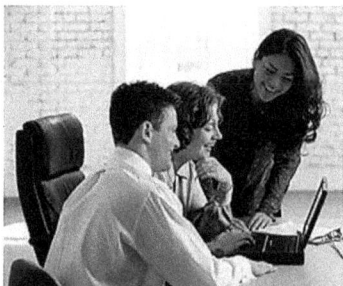

The decision-making process is one that has to be taken wisely, and I will not forget to stress the importance that this process carries. I say this to remind everyone not to be in a hurry in making the decision of purchasing a home. There is one thing that you cannot overlook and that is location. There is a real estate slogan that says," location, location, location" the slogan still bears true today. Location is very crucial. Location means where the property is situated. You might want to look into things like Schools in the area. How close do you want to live to a school? What about churches in the area, if you are a church person, of which, I hope you are!! Look on the activities that take place in the neighborhood. It is possible it could be a nice property, but the location might not be very charming. How far is the property from your work place? You should decide how far you are willing to commute to and from work. I knew of a couple that purchased their home and after they moved in, they started complaining about how far they have to travel to work. They did not plan on of going back to work after they closed on the property, but after finding out that their funds were depleted, they realized they had to go back to work. Don't let this happen to you. You might be wondering why location is so crucial in purchasing a home, the answer is, there is a great deal of money involved, and you do not want to spend it today and regret it tomorrow, that is why the word location is being repeated.

No one enters into real estate to lose money; every one purchases real estate with some hopes of making more money whether it is buying a home to live in or to rent. No one is going to purchase a home for (100,000) one hundred thousand dollars and a few months later puts that property up for sale and ask (75,000) seventy-five thousand dollars. This would be worse than the man that Jesus gave the one talent, he dug the earth and hid the Lord's money instead of investing it so he could bring forth more money, he brought in the same as he was given. Of course, Jesus' remarks were," thou slightly servant" that means he was not wise. We purchase real estate to make money and so should you. After all that I have seen in the real estate business, why I have decided to place this book into your hands, hoping you will take advantage of it, and be not mistaken. Buyers I will be coming to you also, for there are several things that I would like to share with you. I am going to tell you about selling your property, but you will see that in the latter part of my writing to sellers. Once you close on your home, your life goes on with more expenses at hand, and these won't be surprises. The mortgage will have to be paid with all the other bills that come along with buying a home, so make sure that you are ready. Again, we speak of location, and another factor to think of is to make sure the property you are looking at is not sitting in a pond. This could be an important factor regarding your investment. You know what is going to happen when it rains. If you do not have a car and is considering taking public transportation, look on the accessibility to public transportation. These are decisions that

35

need to be addressed. They are to be done before you make the purchase, and by involving the appropriate parties. It is imperative to incorporate all the ideas and thoughts to make your venture an enjoyable and pleasant one. I am encouraging you not to do things and have regrets. What I am doing here is to encourage you to think before you act. This book is an eye opener to those of you who are thinking of venturing into owning your own home. I am not here to scare you, but want you to be an informed person, one that would have some knowledge of what you are entering into. I am assuring you to be a well-informed buyer, whether or not you use a realtor or do it on your own.

Real Estate is fundamental to human existence. It is becoming more and more difficult to own a home, because of the escalating prices in the real estate market. We will agree that the possibility of homeownership is getting harder and harder, think about it. Once you have examined the real estate market you will see for yourself. One thing I have always liked about real estate is, it is truly a win/win, meaning that real the estate transaction is beneficial for everyone involved. The person buying the property wins, the person selling the property wins, the Realtor wins, the bank wins, and down the line. Wherever you are involved you became a winner. Purchasing a home may still be a wise decision, but prospective home buyers should examine the market carefully before they step in it. In this market, buyers and sellers alike need to be informed by experts in the real estate industry. Your thought and consideration should not be ignored because of the complexity of the industry, complex because of the different laws that are involved and needs to be followed.

SHOULD I BUY OR RENT

The question of whether I should buy or rent has been asked on several occasions by a number of prospective home buyers time and time again. I do not know who has the right answer, or who will give the right answer. One thing I know for sure is that after reading this booklet you will be a well-informed person and with such information, you will be able to make an intelligent decision on the matter of home ownership. It does not matter what one might say, what I matter most is who you are and the position that you are in when it comes to owning a home. Many potential buyers go shopping for their first home and might have difficulties, sometimes face different situations so they drop out of the home buying process with an unsure mind of what to do, or if they should continue the process of homeownership. I am not sure if this really brings us to the point of justification that the best thing is to drop out and question the process.

Real Estate transactions can be very complicated if you do not understand what you are about, that is why I encourage you as a first-time home buyer to seek the help of an expert, in this case your expert should be a Realtor. A home purchase is most likely the largest single investment you will ever make. Because it is so costly, few of us are able to make this purchase of buying a home. We are not familiar with the process; therefore, we could get very discourage in experiencing this pain taking process.

A professional that has the know how to get you in and out will put the team together to complete the transaction before the nightmare process begin. There are certain things that we have to look into when we started comparing ownership to renting.

It does not matter what side you are on. Whatever the side you are on you will not know what it is like to be on the other side, unless you were a homeowner. If you were, then you probably know what it is to pay rent, which is why you became a Landlord. Now if you have never purchased real estate before, you would not understand what I am saying so this should give us room to set an appointment. My theory is, you will always need a place to call home, especially if you are a family-oriented person are planning to have a family where you can go and cry, or rejoice whatever your situation might be. The thought of moving each year, or every six months might help you make some intelligent decisions regarding homeownership. This is not a critical decision to make. It is straight down- to-earth intelligence. As I have alluded earlier, moving every six months might help you draw your own conclusion on whether it is better to rent or to purchase. You have very little choice in the matter. You either need a shelter, or you don't whichever way you might choose to satisfy that need. Also, family dedication will play a great role in the ownership decision.

You can decide on a rental which places minimal demand on your time or finances. You can purchase a single-family home, thus taking on all the responsibilities of maintenance and of carrying a home mortgage. Or you may choose to make a smaller purchase like a condominium or a cooperative. Obviously, your choice will, and should, depend on what makes you feel most comfortable. What I am doing here is to point out the various advantage and disadvantages concerning the choices you have. Your personal living will be your choice, but I would like to see you make the best decision in your real estate move.

There are many times we ask questions that we already know the answers, but fail to apply the solution to solve the problem. As a realtor, I have seen many people coming to me asking for an apartment to live, some have outlined that this move is the third in a twelve-month period. Now why wouldn't such person buy a home once they can afford to move three times in one year? What I am going to say here might help you to come to a quicker decision that ownership is better than renting. I would like my readers to do things because of one thing; we call that thing (within) what is in it for me! What I am saying here is that you purchase a home because of what is in that home for you. What's there is the peace of mind that you won't have to move any time soon. This will only happen if you are a candidate for home ownership. I think you should examine yourself first to see which side you would like to be on before you make that move.

As you might have expected, the home ownership rate for a specific group have declined widely, but I urge you not to give in to statistics or what one might think, you have to live somewhere, so why not own the castle that you live in. Intelligently, I have realized that some things are in it for you. The knowledge and the experience you will have gained will be worth it, and not only that but the financial reward will be so too. There is what we call peace of mind. Peace of mind is when you are able to go to sleep knowing that the roof over your head is yours and will be there at all times without unwanted interruptions.

When you leave for work you will return not to find an eviction notice under your door because the Landlord does not like you any more for some unknown reason and would like to see you go. Now I think this is enough reason for you to want to own your home and not wanting to rent. Home ownership is an intelligent investment for yourself that you will see multiplying itself as time goes by. The home you purchase today will worth a lot more tomorrow. Does this make sense to you seeing your money increasing? If this makes sense, then you need no one to solve the equation for you that is quite distinct and clear.

I could remember at the age of eighteen when I owned my first home. I did not question any one or myself whether or not I should own the roof over my head or if I should rent it. Common sense told me that was the intelligent choice. Why at age eighteen? I know I needed a place to call home and a permanent roof over my head not a temporary one. I knew that I would be having a family, and it would be my responsibility to secure a home for them to live. I knew that procrastination would not do the job for me, so I went ahead and did the things I thought best, 'I became a home owner'. I stopped thinking, and took a significant step. Owning your home has some significance to it and you will never know until it happens. Unless you have the desire of home ownership you will not strive to own your home.

When I speak of home ownership, I am not saying that you have to go and purchase something that you cannot afford.

If you do not know what to do or when to start thinking of ownership, what you should do is to meet with a Real Estate professional and by the time they are through with you there will be no doubts left in your mind. You do not have to own a large home for the first, but start small. When I say small, I mean it could be with a condominium, or some people start with a cooperative, if you learn to own then guess what? You are going to continue until you own the entire block. Ownership has to start somewhere and at some point, or the other, so why not let it start with you. There is nothing to lose but your hard-earned money going to some one that is a better thinker than you are. (a landlord)

There are some things that you need to know about ownership. It gives peace of mind that you will not be moving tomorrow. You become the owner of your castle, everyone is proud and that is what you call equity building in your home, and equity means money for those of you that do not know what equity is. I have not yet told you what it is but I will do so shortly. From what I have said so far, why wouldn't you want to purchase a home knowing that it is yours, and you could live there as long as you are paying the mortgage. You know if you don't pay, or you are not willing to pay, then you would have to move when the bank steps in, so make sure you pay up that is my tip to you.

Why rent when you can buy? This is a question frequently ask by realtors. For those who are renting, I know when you read this book you will be finding the realtor in your neighborhood. You rent only because you do not know better, but now your thoughts have changed, you know better so you will be doing better. You do not want to be moving twice per year, when rent has escalated so much, but most of all, look what has happened to your money. You have a family of one girl and a boy; you need a three-bed room apartment to rent. Let us be conservative since I do not know what part of the country you are living. A three bedroom could be $ 1000. Some places may be less, while other places are more, so we are splitting thin airs right know. Paying $1000 per month for rent, one year would equal $12,000 and say you live there for five years, my calculation gives me $60,000 that would add up to sixty pieces of receipt that you have to either take with you for souvenirs that have no good memories or throw in the garbage, taking into consideration, no rent increase for five years if you could find that landlord. All these receipts that you have collected, they simply have no value whatsoever, so now you decide if renting is equivalent to purchasing your own home. If you were created to think logically, no one needs to guide you into home ownership we call this simple economics. Look at it, there are so many things we know but we do not put them into practice, which became very costly over a period of time. We procrastinate while time rolls on, not realizing that time waits for no one, and while we wait, we are losing money, so why wait? There is more to lose in waiting than to gain, so take control of your destiny.

There is not plenty of land that is left to be developed, so if you have seen short sighted people telling you that there is time enough to do whatever you wanted, the interesting news you will have to counteract is that, "time waits on no man". Stop and think about it for a moment. If you have ever seen an old building of any kind, you will notice sooner or later someone will take that old run-down property and restore it. We have to learn to restore the things that are in demand, and in this case, we refer to real estate. What I am saying here is, over the years you have not seen the importance of owning your home, or to invest in real estate, you have not taken on a positive attitude, but rather that of procrastinator, instead of taking advantage of the opportunities when they present themselves. The land is not increasing, look around you, you will see what is increasing, in case you are not reading your newspaper, or watching your nightly news. These sources give the vital information necessary to catch up with the happenings around us. In case you do not see or read about it I am telling you. I have told you, every day there are more and more people adding to modern earth. We called this population growth while the land remains the same, what this means is that one day someone will be left without a place to live. Don't be short change, opportunity waits for no one.

When we speak of buying versus renting, each person has their own idea. Renting might be cheaper if it is looked on in the short term. Owning your own home has more to offer in the long term, as you read on you will pick up on this. If we look on this on a individual basis, you will know what makes you comfortable. In a way that could be true, but there are times we made ourselves comfortable in some things that are not really edifying or make sense, and some of the things we do, do not profit anything. Most of my readers will agree with me. If I could make my personal assessment on this, I would think that we should look on the advantages and disadvantage concerning ownership for you and your family.

When you can clearly and honestly distinguish the advantages from the disadvantages, it will make the world of difference, and then you will see whether or not you are a candidate for home ownership. At this point you should well be on the way to a careful planning and giving thoughtful consideration to what you should be doing to acquire your first property. Once you understood the process it will be very much easier to get in, so you can become more familiar with the process. I have seen so many potential home buyers want to own their first home, but they are scared to death to take the first move, but remember, if you do not start there will not be an end. There is absolutely nothing to be afraid of, but saving money and getting some equity on your investment is more money for you and your family.

WHAT IS AN EQUITY?

We have often times heard the word Equity mentioned, but what is Equity? Does everyone have Equity? The answer is clearly NO. For someone to have equity, that person has to own a home. One day my phone wrong, when I picked it up a Lady was on the other end, she asks me "How can I use my equity? I asked her, where is your home? Her reply was, I do not have a home. Sorry, you do not have equity. For someone to have equity, you have to own a piece of property. You have to be a home owner. Equity is earned through the acquisition of a property. For instance, you bought a property two years ago for one hundred and fifty thousand dollars. Today the property is worth four hundred thousand dollars. What happen is, the property went up in value two and fifty hundred thousand dollars. These two hundred and fifty thousand dollars is in the property, you can go to a lending institution and tell them that you have a home that worth four hundred thousand dollars, in return, they are going to ask you, how much is owed on the property? The amount that is owed will determine the equity that is there for you. Unless you take that equity from the property in the form of cash it will stay there until you sell the property. Once it stays in the property, it doing absolutely nothing. You can use this money to anything of your choice, whether it be shopping for a new car, or a vacation. There is still one smart thing to do. Look what is going to happen in this formula. There is two hundred and fifty thousand dollars sitting in your home. Take two hundred thousand dollars in the form of equity from the home. That money can be used to purchase other two homes. One hundred thousand per property, now, you are the owner of three properties. Because Real Estate price goes up each month or say every six months. The first home you had gone up to a whapping four hundred and fifty thousand dollars. The two second homes went up also to three hundred and fifty thousand dollars. Now let's look on your property value, $450,000first home, two second home purchase with equity $350,000 plus $350,000 gives a total of over 1.1 million in two smart investments. Now let us look back on how much money was invested in all. On the first home was purchase for one hundred and fifty thousand dollars. The other two homes were at one hundred thousand each, let's say there were repairs totaling one hundred and fifty thousand dollars, there is still six hundred thousand dollars remaining in your pocket. Although all this did not happen over knight, you could give yourself, say, five years on, because you need to learn, and to know when to take action. What a wonderful leverage in home owner ship. "I call this the milking cow" so, why wouldn't you want to own your home and stop paying rent. If this pattern should be duplicated a few times, the outcome would be astronomical. This is why we said, knowledge is power, and if utilized, will bring tremendous changes. Once the necessary improvements are made to a property, it will continue to build the equity you need to excel and build wealth. Too many times people think there is a magic in excelling in Real Estate. There is no magic neither is it a mystery. What you want out of Real Estate that is what you are going to put in. I believe the words of Shakes pear when he said, "life is what you make it to be". Believe it or not, equity created in your home is a win- win situation. The lenders love it, and the owners are happy, because, they are making money.

BUYING A NEW HOME

You may be considering buying a new home, nothing is wrong with buying a new home if you can afford it, as you know a new home may be a little more expensive than an older home. If you are considering a new home here are some tips to consider, you should investigate the builder thoroughly. You may call your local consumer affairs office or the housing division in your county, as well as the better business bureau to see if any complaints have been lodged against the builder, and if so, how did the builder address the problem.

One thing to keep in mind is that not all consumers or buyers file complaints. It would be necessary to visit the different communities where the company recently built homes, the closer the community is to where you want to build your home the better, those are the ones you should be interested in. You want to make sure someone is at home for you to talk with so, pick your time to make these visits. I would recommend that you go on a Saturday morning when you know most people are home, and may be doing a little gardening, they will be outside, so you will see them. Randomly ask the people what their experience were with their builder. They will tell you, although some might be somewhat curious at first, wanting to know why you are asking such question, but don't be afraid to let them know that you are considering moving into the neighborhood, and are looking for a builder to build your home. Once you explain as the night follows the day, they will give you the information you are looking for. When you are satisfied and decided on the contractor you will be using, then you should get into an agreement with the builder.

Remember to read your contract carefully if there are terms that you do not like or understand don't overlook them or take it for granted that it is all right, consult someone that know better, or show it to your Attorney. Your builder might try to convince you that you can sign, that it is a standard contract, but take nothing for granted. Where there are doubts, check it out. Be not mistaken, if there are things in the contract that you do not like, point them out to the contractor. It is possible you can re-negotiate and it can be changed. The only thing that matter is, that both parties in the contract agree on the changes.

I remember reading an article written by a famous attorney that says "If you fail to negotiate a contract, shame on you." Some builders may want to take away virtually every important legal right that a homebuyer would want to have. You should make sure you get what you're asking for in writing, it won't hurt one bit. There are many advantages in purchasing a new home. You will have the builder's warrantee, maintenance free for five to ten years. For sure, you will have the enjoyment of your home for long time maintenance free, but you might have to pay a little more in cost. This does not prevent you from asking for what you want. It is best you ask and don't get it, then to know you would have gotten some kind of a bargain, only if you had asked. "Shame on you if you don't ask", I have seen many people lose so much in their transactions only because they fail to ask for what they wanted. Don't fall into that category. Remember "shame on you if you don't ask."

Be an informed buyer, it is your responsibility to get the information you need regarding the purchasing of your home. Be sure that what you purchase is satisfactory in every respect. You have the right to carefully examine your potential new home with a qualified home inspector. You may do so before the signing of your final contract as long as your contract states that the sale of the home depends on the inspection. I would like to inform you that you should get your own home inspection. There is nothing that says you have to go with the inspector that is given to you.

Whenever you purchase a property that needs improvement, steps should be taken to hire a good home inspector. This person is a specialist who specializes in home inspection and will do a thorough job for you to put your mind at ease when you move in. He will spot potential problems and provide you with the condition of the home and even give you a detailed list of the present condition including the equipment's that are in the home. I think without a professional home inspector; you are leaving yourself wide open for potential problems that could be avoided in the future. The home buying process could be a complex one and should not be taken lightly because, once you are closed, it's you and your home.

Remember, you cannot walk away and leave it, you must make sure you can live with it in the years to come. My suggestion is, spend $450.00 to secure your $350,000 in investment; smart, isn't it?

MAKING YOUR OFFER

If you are successful in finding your home, now it's time to submit your offer. Sound scary, isn't it? Actually, it's not really scary. Discuss the offering process with your real estate agent and he will take care of that for you. If it is possible, ask your agent to spend some time with you so he or she could discuss the offering process clause by clause. This would give you the full understanding of the process. There might be some issues that you probably would like your agent to address with you before the submission of your offer. You should make sure that your offer is contingent upon the property upraising at its full sales value, and upon you being able to qualify for a loan as set forth in the purchase agreement. Also, make sure that the date of possession of the property is clearly written so that you know when to plan for moving into your new home. The dates that are written in the agreement are up to change, if you notice you will see the wording of your contract goes like this "on or about the 15th June 2003" which means that the date is not definite. Sometimes the banks might have issues, an attorney might be out of town, or the title company might be over booked, you never know what might happen since it's a long process that is involved with a lot of people. No one can really hold the other to the date that was first mentioned. That is why it says on or about. Remember, in a contract you can change things as long as both parties agree.

I know you might want to give your current landlord a 30 days' notice that you will be moving, but since your landlord already purchased a home, he or she knows and understand the process. You just have to let them know that this was a projecting date and is not written in stone. So, it is proper to inform your landlord. Your attorney might assist you of when you should notify your landlord. Treat him the way you would like to be treated, because you are now a landlord and want to be treated respectfully and correctly. The other thing you might want to do is to make arrangement for your utilities to be turned on in your name in the new home, but don't get alarmed, you will be guided through the process as time progresses. Once you are ready to make the offer, I know you will be asking your agent the various steps to be taken, such as, how much should you offer, but let me tell you, there is no standard amount that should be offered on a property. Every situation is different. The property that is overpriced will more than likely receive a lower price than the property that is underpriced or the one that is rightly priced. A good question for you to ask your agent is "How long has the property been on the market. What is the seller's motivation?" Is it in foreclosure or is a job transfer, or to buy a new home? Find out if the agent knows of any recent sales in the area for the past six months in the same neighborhood with similar square footage and bedrooms? This is called (CMA) comparable sales. This alone will give you a good indication as to what a property will eventually sell for. Another question you should ask, is it a buyers' market? I do not think that will help you much because your agent would have already done a CMA and know about what the property should have sold for. Are there other offers on the property, you might want to know that. If there are other offers that mean you might have to come closer to asking price. The exception to this is if you are buying for investment or you are purchasing to live.

ACCEPTING YOUR OFFER

For your offer to be accepted, there are some things that will be considered such as percentage down and closing costs. Sometimes the offer has to have some attraction if you want it go through. Definitely, the exception to this is, if there is a cash buyer, he or she would get the first chance of acceptance, if they do not take disadvantage of the sale because they are paying cash that would be too bad. Unless the buyer or buyers do not know they have more buying paying cash. I have seen this happen many times. A cash buyer will walk in and say I am paying cash, so he offers fifty thousand below asking price, again I will not say that it will not work, it depends heavily on the situation of the seller.

One thing I know, cash will give the exception to get your offer accepted if it is genuine. It could bring lower price, why? The seller does not have to wait for a long time to close the sale. He would not have to wait until the purchaser obtains a mortgage from a bank, because of the quick sale he or she will settle for a couple of thousand less than the asking price. The seller will be quicker to accept if it is a cash sale, meaning, you the buyer have all the money sitting in your account and is ready to close within two weeks once the title work is done. This is called a cash deal. Another banging tool is a large down payment. Most sellers do ask about the amount of down payment when they get an offer, bigger the down payment the more solid the deal becomes, and sellers do look into it also, they want to know that once the property is taken off the market the sale is substantiating. I am not saying that this happen, but when I am the seller, I ask about the credit, most sellers leave that to the lending institution, but this is the reason why some deals do not go to the closing the time they should. If you want your offer to be accepted, you have to let it look presentable, what do I mean by presentable? A home is selling for $250,000 (two hundred and fifty thousand) the offer is made for $200,000 with a credit score of 560 and 2.5% down, the buyer is looking for some closing concession, now this would be a drowning seller to go after these conditions. There is just no attraction to this sale and a knowledgeable agent might not want to present this kind of an offer, the terms are just not good. An offer on a property does not mean the sellers will accept, they will come back with what is called a counter offer, meaning the sale price is $250,000 you made an offer of $200,000 the seller could come back and say I will accept $248,000 or say, I am not going below my asking price of $250,000. Now you would have to decide if you take it for the $250 or you go looking for another home, but what I know is, it would depend on how much you like the property and of course the condition it's in.

Once you accept the counter offer and the seller agrees on the terms and condition that your agent has presented on your behalf, you will have to go into a contract. But bear in mind that the seller can sell the property to someone else, there is nothing to say the property cannot go to another buyer, because technically there is not a written agreement, because there is nothing in writing. Your agent will guide you through the process while you continue to experience the road of becoming a landlord.

I heard someone say, you eat an elephant one bite at a time. By taking all of these steps and action, you are getting closer and closer to owning your home. You see each step that you have taken is getting you there. In other words, you are gaining momentum. However, there are still more to be accomplished, but we will get there as time progresses.

BUYERS GUIDE

Congratulations! You have decided to purchase, or thinking of purchasing your home.

You will be joining hundreds of families who realize that home ownership offers a number of benefits including building equity, financial stability, creating wealth and on environment to earning power. The equity you earn on your home will increase, and it is yours to keep. Following, you will find information which makes a wise buying decision. We will take you through the planning process step by step, to help you determine if the home you are looking at is the right home for you. You will find a host of different mortgage information, and how you could calculate your own monthly mortgage payment. Including are information on making and accepting offers. Make good use of the information as it will be of great help to you in the process.

A buyer does look behind a cluttered apartment. A famous writer once said "a product must have dust to be of value" think about it. Some minor cleaning or repairs could help you gain substantial equity in your purchase. Whether you are a first-time buyer or a repeated buyer, your aim is to get the best possible deal on the market. The bottom line why people buy Real Estate is to make money. You will only make money when you buy wisely. I am trying to help you become a savvy buyer by pointing out some of the inherent in the home buying process. Buying your home should be a smooth step by step process that should not be emotional nor overly time consuming.

I would like for everyone to avoid the most common errors in the buying process, and those made by most buyers. Whatever you do, avoid the emotions and trust your Realtor he or she is the expert that will help make the process go as fast and as smoothly as possible. I warn you because some buyers get overwhelmed and excited when buying their first home. Whenever this happen, important areas will be over looked, and will be only discovered when it is too late. If you have a systematic plan before you shoot, you are sure to avoid costly errors. Most errors occur with renters who are purchasing their first home, without highlighting the different factors that should be considered when purchasing said home.

In this market buyers and sellers alike need, be informed by experts in the Real Estate industry. This does require thoughts because of the complexity of the industry. It is complex because of the different laws that govern the market. When we speak of different laws, we are looking at the (IRS.) Internal Revenue Service, (HUD.) Department of Housing Urban Development, (FHA.) federal Housing Administration, (VA.) Veterans Affair, and the (EPA.) Environmental Protection Agency. The role of Government has helped to regulate the and influence the real estate industry. This industry a whole has been the backbone of the economy, if the real estate market is down, then naturally the economy will be bad, and this has been proven over the years.

INCREASE YOUR PROPERTY VALUE

There are some techniques that sellers should know when they are selling their properties. I would recommend sellers do some kind of repairs, those that are within limit, and that are reasonable. Some sellers do things that are not necessary, or reasonable.

It would be good if the necessary things are done to the property before it goes on the market, if these are done, it will ensure you the buyer of a higher price and a faster sale. Too much money should not be spent for improvement, you might not recapture those monies. You do not have to put a whole lot of money in to get it sold, or because you want to over price the property. Just do the necessary repairs and give it a good coat of paint with a good color, not black!! If a homeowner puts a lot of money in repairs for selling the property, he or she might not be able to capture all the monies after the sale that is called over improvement. Therefore sellers, be careful whenever you are going to do repairs on your home to put it on the market, seek the help of an expert if you are not sure what to do.

Relocation has to be well thought of once your home is on the market. You have to think of cost in relocating, value is of some importance in the sale of your home. It has to be clear in your mind when determining the amount of dollar to be spent on your home before putting it on the market. Not all monies that are spend for improvement will improve the property and add value, for instance, building a pool will not add value. It is possible the buyer does not want a pool. I had an instance once where the property I was selling had a pool and the prospective buyer did not want a pool. The seller wanted the sale to go through so he agreed to dump the pool. Not all modification will add value. An improper finished porch without a permit will not add value. Another good example, is adding two bedrooms to an existing two bedrooms home with only one bath room, no closet space will definitely add some square feet, but little or no value would be added to the property. If you are thinking of making certain repairs or addition to your home you should check with the municipality in the town in which you live, they will give their approval for the work to be done. Otherwise, it could create a nightmare for you when you are ready to put it on the market.

I do not want to deviate from the topic of increasing your property value. Increasing of property value has to do with the conformity of other homes in the area. For example, if an improvement is done on a home that is next to a gas station or a semitary you might just find out that you have wasted some money. This is because the improvement cost that was put in will not be recaptured. The home might be looking good, but its location does not warrant the improvement that was made to it. There are other scenarios to be considered when it comes to improving your home.

INCREASE YOUR CREDIT SCORE

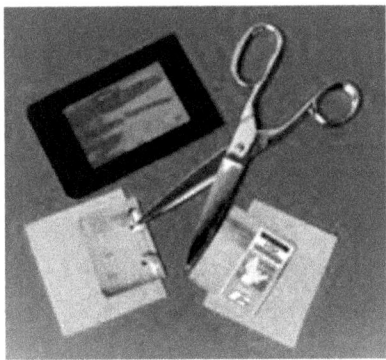

There are many people that do not know what a credit score is, or its effect regarding making a purchase, whether it is a home or a car or anything that has to do with credit.

Credit scores are very important when you are trying to secure a loan to complete a purchase. You might want to know what your credit score says about you before you even start the process of buying. There are many that ask, what does a credit score has to do with me buying a house? A good credit score plays a major role in the process of a home, if the buyer is going to secure a loan from a lending institution. Once you are thinking of buying, a good thing to do is to check your credit before to see what it says about you. The reason for this is if the credit is bad, there will be time to correct what is there. It might take months to clear it up, but by doing it early it gives you enough time, and there will not be surprises, you would be ahead of the game, and not only so but you will be glad you did.

Another good thing an early start on your credit would do is give you time to build your credit score if needed. If you are not comfortable with your score and want to build it you can. Let's say for instance your score is 580 and you want to build the score to 6 20 which is acceptable by most lending institutions. You have a credit card with $150, one with $85, and say a visa have $300 plus a couple of late payments, these are going to give you a low score. You should pay the $85, if possible, pay the $150, and then write a letter of explanation stating your situations and, why you were late to some degree, maybe you were dead!! But now you are alive and well, and want to pay your depths the Company will be glad to get the letter, but they still want the money. This would leave you in a good position to increase your credit scores. It is possible you might not be able to pay all what is owed, so pay the smaller ones. The total amount you owed on credit card would be $ 535. What you are doing is building your credit score so you will be able to get a higher score to impress your lending institution. So, by you paying some, or all what was owed, your score is going to change from 580 to say 620 or may be 680 which would be the perfect score to obtain a mortgage. This could lower your monthly payment significantly and save you thousands of dollars on your mortgage over the years. Now it is clear why you should look into your credit before you are actually ready to approach your bank for a loan. I would like to give you a couple of hints to preserve your credit when you get into your home, (1) pay your bills on time, late payment leaves bad taste in your mouth and can be very serious for you. Try to avoid too much enquires in your credit report, enquires will hurt you. (3) Do not apply for too much credit card at once, you could be choked. (4) Reduce credit card balance as much as possible, maxed out credit card is bad for your health!! Don't do it. (5) Establish and maintain 3-4 pieces of good credit in your name, when you get them, treat them well they will pay off later.

In cases where you cannot purchase by yourself, you might have to use a co-signer, A co-signer could be a brother, a sister, father, mother, or even a friend, one that has a job, and a fairly decent credit. The co-signer would have to do the same things as you have done. Check that the credit has a fairly decent report, have a job, and be qualified just the way in which you did. Your co-signer does not have to come up with a deposit, you are the owner of the property, therefore the down payment is your responsibility. If this is a joint venture then it will be something different.

HOME OWNERS TIPS

For some people a home isn't just a roof over their head, but a financial investment as well. Home prices are usually not as volatile as the stock market, though each home may vary accordingly to local market conditions. In recent years, record home sales along with home value appreciation and home equity loans have helped boost the North America economies.

According to a recent report issued by the National Association of realtors in the U.S. Six out of ten homeowners have more home equity built into their homes than the wealth of the stock market. Statistics shows that homeownership rate in 2004 was 68%, while only 52% own stocks. Total housing consumption operation related goods and investments accounts for about 23% of the U.S. gross domestic product in the year 2003. Many homeowners regard their home as a wise investment that appreciates in price and even provide a system for automatic saving through mortgage payments. A homeowner can access the wealth invested in their home through a home equity line of credit or loan. If you can afford it consider making an extra payment on the principal of your loan to help shorten the time it would normally take to pay off your thirty-year mortgage. You would be building more equity into your property home as you make those extra payments.

THE BASICS MAKING AN OFFER

The basis of making an offer is to show interest in the property. Making the offer opens the door for negotiation with the seller and the buyer through the agent. In most cases this is done in a written format. A written proposal is the foundation of a real estate transaction. Oral promises are not legally enforceable when it comes to the sale of real estate. Therefore, you need to enter into a written proposal. The proposal not only specifies price, but all the terms and conditions of the purchase. For example, if the sellers said they will help with $3,000 towards your closing cost, be sure to include that in your offer and also in the completed contract, or you won't have grounds for the challenge later to say here is a $3,000 concession if it is not in writing.

Again, your real estate agent will usually have a variety of standard forms, these including residential purchase agreement, and others that are kept up to date with different changes and laws. Your agents also will question and put in place those things that are needed to be addressed during the process of compiling the contract. Recently, some states have drawn up disclosure laws that have to be completed by the seller when listing the property for sale. Your real estate agent will present it to you, so you will look it over. Now that there is an offer of acceptance you will need an attorney. You could read this book over and over, but not until you get out and get some experience, will you really know what I am talking about. We call this practical hands-on experience. This is just the beginning of your real estate journey. I do not want you to think that this will be the only book you will see on real estate, but for sure, this will be the only one written in this manner. If you are to be successful, you have to start from somewhere. This is your starting point. This is the biggest investment you'll ever make, with long term financial ramifications. It calls for many informal decisions and for good advice from a real estate professional. Whether working with the buyer or the seller, Realtors pledge to provide fair and ethical treatment for all parties in the transactions. Here are some ways working with a Realtor will work for you in terms of your convenience, your budget, and your overall satisfaction. Put your Realtors to the test, they will work honestly for you.

WHY DO I NEED AN ATTORNEY

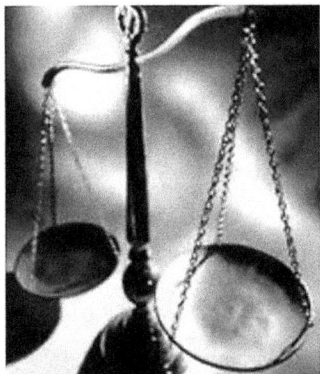

You may ask the question as many others have asked. "Do I really need a real estate attorney? There are things that you need to do that you just cannot do for yourself because you are spending your life's earning, you should engage an attorney to look over what you are doing. Believe me, you will not lose instead you will gain, and will be glad you did. Once both parties accept the offer, the next step is to draw up a contract of sale and that should be done by the attorney, although in some states, your agent can do the contract and then present it to the attorney for an overview, but it is better to leave each specialist in their areas. You will need your attorney to give you advice as you continue through the process of accomplishing the property of your dream. Your attorney has to communicate with the seller's attorney and sometimes with your finance company. He has to do your title work which ensures that you are getting a good title to your property, so he will be working for you. A very important part of the process is that you will not understand until you go to closing, but with a real estate attorney, you have nothing to worry about so trust your attorney. He knows what he is doing. By the way, if you do not know a real estate attorney, don't be afraid to say you do not know one; your agent knows many real estate attorneys and could give you several to choose from.

The attorney is the person that will look out for you and your money; and look over your contract. If he is not the one that draws up the contract, he will guide you through the process, although you might have done so with your realtor earlier. The process of buying a home is of such that you will need all the relevant information possible.

Your Attorney do the title work and will do the relevant paper work that is needed before you go to the closing. In other words, he sees you through the closing. Once your closing is completed, you will know if you are comfortable with that attorney, if so, you may want to keep him as your real estate attorney, you are now a landlord you might need an Attorney as you pursue your real estate dream him later. This is your real estate journey that you have started so keep your attorney by your side. A good Attorney will always look out for the client, so once you find one you should keep him or her.

EARNEST MONEY DEPOSIT

What is an earnest money deposit? This is a question asked by many potential buyers. We will try to give an explanation of this earnest money deposit. I can remember on several occasions I had people coming to me saying, they would like to purchase a home. After talking with them, I found out they are having a good intention wanting to purchase, but they are not ready. Most of the potential buyers that I have spoken with are thinking of borrowing Fifteen Thousand Dollars ($15, 000.00) or Twenty Thousand Dollars ($20, 00.00) to deposit in their savings account to use as deposit upon purchasing a home.

To all you potential buyers, it does not work like that. Earnest money deposit is money which is saved over the years and has reached a sizeable amount so it can be a deposit on a home. Your bank would want to see a pattern of saving before they actually give you a mortgage. There cannot be a deposit of Ten Thousand Dollars ($10, 000.00) one month and another deposit of Ten Thousand Dollars ($10,000.00) another month. These large deposits may not be verifiable, neither can they be traced, they can trigger an investigation. You will not be able to use these funds to purchase a home. You cannot make these large deposits, at the same time, you are on a job that pays minimum wage, or your income is ($500) five hundred dollars per week. It just will not work.

What you have to realize is that the bank is trusting you in giving you a loan of 98% of the total value of the home. For example, if the home is Two Hundred and Fifty Thousand Dollars ($250, 000.00) you are making a deposit of 3% which is Seven Thousand, Five Hundred Dollars ($7,500.00), that means the bank has more interest in the home than you have. Look at it, your investment in the property is a mere Seven Thousand, Five Hundred Dollars ($7,500.00) versus the banks interest of $242, 500. Now because of this amount the bank has paid to the seller on your behalf, the bank has to make sure that you are in a good position to repay the loan on a monthly and timely basis.

This payment can only be done when you have a job and is receiving a regular income form that job. Secondly, they want to know that you have fairly good credit. I have spoken to many people who ask me how they can get good credit. This is how you get good credit rating. You apply for (1) a credit card from a bank or store or (2) borrow any money from a recognized lending institution and repay that loan on a timely basis. The institution from which you get the money will give a report of payment history to the credit bureaus and this will become your permanent record for future references. As much time as you do this, the information will be compiled, so in essence you determine your credit history and what is on your credit report.

The third thing that is required by the lending institution is, the buyer has to have a savings account in which he makes regular deposits until the account grows. In this manner your funds are traceable, it shows consistency in savings. Making the deposits when you are decided to purchase is not a good decision to make. And be not misunderstood, the banks are going to find out before they give you the money. Or even before they go into a contract for the loan. Once you show interest in applying to a lending institution for a loan, one of the first thing they will require will be your name, and then your social security number, which is going to tell them a lot about you the applicant, after the bank has done its finding, they will determine whether or not the loan will be granted. You may not know why you have to give this information, but as I have told you early, they want to see if you are really ready to purchase. If you are thinking of purchasing a home, a good thing to do is to get a credit report before you are ready and you will see what is on it. If you cannot read it, ask someone to help you, and if the scores are low ask someone who you think might know what you can do to improve the score so that they would be higher.

Some lending institutions are very strict on credit scores. Many would not get into a transaction with you if the scores are below 5 00, while some will consider you. Lending institutions rate your scores A to D. What they do is equate the number with a letter which would give you your credit score. "A" is very good and might be over 700. D might be 450 and would give you a very hard time to negotiate a loan with some lending institutions. So, if you want to get an approval from your bank you would have to keep your credit score up. If they are not up, you will have to start working on getting these scores up. Maybe by paying off some credit cards or turning in some of the cards you are holding, or have the card company close these accounts, you will be surprised the difference these things will have make on your credit report. If you do not need 10 or 12 credit cards, why carry them? You are just setting yourself up for trouble. If you cannot do with two cards, then you should start thinking again. You may need to do some adjusting in your spending. Credit cards are the instrument to poverty when you cannot afford them. Worst of all, you will have to control your spending habits.

WHAT IS A HOME?

No one has ever stopped to look on the privileges they have in owning a home, or to question themselves or any one as to what a home really is, or why we save our monies and later used it to purchase a home. So, let us look into home ownership as to what a home really is. A home is the place where the family resides. It is the place where the children are raised in a Godly atmosphere. A home is the place where we share the joy of life with the family. Once you are away from home, there will be that feeling of wanting to be home. It is a place, where we laugh, cry, and make our feelings known. We often refer to this place as "home sweet home."

God has given to every man a desire to have a shelter or a over our heads. Man has to live somewhere, in Genesis it speaks of the bird having a nest, but the son of man has no place to lay his head. A home does not have to be a castle, or a palace, neither does it have to be as a No Man's Land, it could be a mansion with a limited amount of square feet, but it is home. Many times, we strive for things we could do without, and that, which does not satisfy the soul or the body, but for sure, having a place to call home, is some kind of relief to an everlasting desire. A home does not necessarily have to be luxurious, but it can be a place where the family lives and the presence of the Lord dwells within it. In Joshua 24:15, Joshua speaks of his intention regarding himself and his household, he states, "As for me and my house, we will serve the Lord." Such profound words spoken which means that a home is a place of refuge, you can have peace of mind, seek renewed strength daily and have a closer relationship with God. Whether your home is large or small, it should be filled with the grace and peace of God. We should let our home be a place of triumph where the Spirit of God dwells at all times. In my thirty (30) years of home ownership, I have learned how to appreciate the blessings of God towards my family and myself. I would like to pass this legacy of blessings onto my friends, co-workers, families and as many that will read this book. I think this is a lesson well needed to be learned.

I truly think that, when you are looking for something, you will find it. If you are scared, you will surely lose what you are looking for. 'Knowledge is Power' and it should not be wasted; if utilized properly, it will be passed on to future generations. One has to have adequate planning which is in three (3) stages, (1) ownership (2) building wealth and (3) enjoying what you have accumulated. I am a great advocate of homeownership; many have heard me speaking on this subject time and time again and it bears true to this day. My family, sometimes think I am crazy and about to lose my head, and they sometimes raise their eyebrows at me when they hear me speaking about Real Estate and homeownership, but I just cannot contain myself. I do have a passion for Real Estate; it is the right thing to do. As a professional in the Real Estate industry over the years, I have seen a lot. The trend comes and goes, and yes, sometimes come back again. The Real Estate market fluctuates at times, but it is here to stay. Real Estate is not getting cheaper, but is getting more expensive to own property. So do not delay or put off the chance of homeownership, get focused, you will not regret it, but will be blessed in the end.

FINDING A BARGAIN

This is very important in the real estate industry; everyone is looking for a bargain and is asking "Where can I find a bargain?" Nothing is wrong with finding bargains if they are around and are available. There are always bargains out there, but it is just for you to find them. Most time others find it before you do, but keep looking, your time will come. Good bargains do not come easily. That does not mean they are not out there, but it is a matter of time. If you are a first-time home buyer, with limited amount of funds, finding a bargain can be a bit difficult and could take you a long time to run into that gold mine. Unless you have an elderly neighbor that own for a very long time and now wants to get out, your future could be next door.

Trying to find a bargain does not come easily, so when you are looking for one, try to maintain a very neutral attitude. If you get emotionally involved in any buying decision, it may sway you too much and there would be the possibility of you making a wrong decision. I always tell my buyers never fall in love with a property, and if they do, I do not want to know, and please do not show it. Why? It could lead you into trouble. I am not saying bargains are not good, but with love, emotions and a little cash to work with, can spell trouble, when in doubt, consult an expert.

Bargains can lead to big profit, there is no doubt about that. I am not saying it will not happen, but wrong approach, and excitement can shatter that dream and once your potential gold mine becomes a bag of sand, you will get discouraged and will be very unwilling to try again. I remember talking to a purchaser, who because of the love and emotion he had for the property at the time he over paid for it. After about fifteen years the home was not worth the price it was bought for years ago.

Once the seller knows you love his home, why should he negotiate with you? You see what you are looking for so pay the price. My theory is, the home is in good condition but there has to be at least two things that you can find to say about it. I do not know what your two things will be you will have to find them. They are not made in heaven, so there has to be more than two things about it that you can discredit to save yourself some money.

You know the seller will be telling you all the good things about buying their home, but if you are like me, the more they tell, the less I want to pay for the property. I am not saying you are to use my strategy as it may not work for you, because it might be hard for you to support your claim. That would make it more difficult to complete the sale if it is something that you would like to have. Notice what I have said "like to have" not that you love the property.

In buying anything, I discredit the word love. In the notion of excitement, I use the word love to someone that has feeling, and can respond when I show love. It is not applicable to anything that will not respond with feelings and emotion. We get excited to see our friends, because in turn they will do the same. What we are getting are two emotions, one begets the other. If we should get excited and emotional in buying, what you think will happen? We are going to fall in love with whatever it is, and the bottom line is the seller is going to see that very quickly. Buying the property with emotion and excitement, wrapped up with love, is too much to pay for a property.

I will attempt to tell you some of the ways to find bargains if you can find the time to exhaust these areas. Tax lean sales are where you probably could find property. These properties will eventually go into foreclosure if the owner does not pay up their taxes. Therefore, the possibility exist that you could pick up a tax lien sale, you would have to check your municipality for such sale. Bankruptcy sales are another avenue that you can use to achieve your goal. These days we find that many people are going into bankruptcy and may want to get out of what they are in. Let us also look into foreclosures. Statistics show that foreclosures will always be around.

Foreclosures usually occur because home owners cannot afford their property any longer, or they just do not want it. In either case, the foreclosure market offers a tremendous opportunity for the buyers if they can cash in on them. Again, you might need the help of a knowledgeable person that knows how to approach these sales to guide you into them. You could make lots of money but without proper knowledge, you could lose lots of money also.

WHEN TO BUY A HOME

I have heard many people question themselves, "Should I purchase a home or should I rent. Most times people try to figure the cheapest way to live. So, it became a roller coaster, should I buy or should I rent than to buy". Let me say it is cheaper to buy than to rent. Although you have to come up front with a lump-sum of cash, but what we are to look at is the long-term gain. I like to sell my first- time buyers two family homes although many of them came to me looking for a one family. With a rod of correction, I will soon drive it far from their minds that one family is good when you can afford it, when you cannot afford a one family, buy a two-family home. Surprising, isn't it?

Most first-time buyers do not know it is cheaper to maintain a two-family home than it is to maintain a one family home. Let us look on a ten year break down. Today you can purchase a two- family home for Two hundred thousand dollars ($200,000.00) a 5% deposit of which is ten thousand dollars ($10,000.00).Take the deposit from the selling price, and the remainder is your mortgage amount you will get from your lending institution which is one hundred and ninety thousand ($190,000.00). There has to be a closing cost, do not try to avoid it, you cannot. We know it is a lot of money, but if you do not have the closing plus the deposit, your bank will allow your seller to give you some closing cost. Each case is different, so ask about sellers' concession for closing, when you are making the offer. In some cases, there can be 100% closing cost financed while in other cases it could be 3%, but if you ask you will get it. "You will always need to negotiate".

Now look at these numbers carefully, they are going to tell you a lot. As I have shown you earlier your mortgage amount is one hundred and ninety thousand ($190,000.00) you will be repaying this money at one thousand two hundred and sixty-four (1,264) per month with an interest rate of 7% for thirty years. This amount does not include taxes and insurance.

They were not included because the numbers vary depending on where you are, the amount of taxes that might be on your property, and again it has to do with where in the country you are. The same goes for your insurance. Now, remember that you have a two-family home and one apartment will be a rental unit. The rented unit will be generating a thousand ($1,000) per month, again depending on the state that you are in, it could be a little more or less your monthly payment however is $1264. There is a rental income of $1,000 take the rental income from your mortgage payment, the remainder is $264 this would be your provision of monthly payment plus your taxes and insurance.

Stop, look at this, your monthly payment is only $264 plus your taxes and insurance. Let's say you are in New York where everything is higher than anywhere else in the U.S. If that is the case, your tax would be $3,000 divided by 12 would give your monthly payment for your taxes which is $250, take the same steps to calculate for your insurance. If your insurance is $800 divided by 12 it would give you $67. Now once you total your portion of the mortgage, your taxes and the insurance, you are looking at $ 581 per month. We would call that out-of-pocket money; that means your home would cost you $581 per month while it cost the tenant $1,000. What happens here is the tenant pays $12,000 of the $15,168 per year that you are supposed to spend for your mortgage, while you the owner picks up the smaller portion of $3,168. The tenant is still paying for the home. That is why I encourage home ownership. I did not look into what tax deductions that you are entitled to, your accountant would do a better job on taxes, which would further reduce your yearly payment. The tenant pays more than what the owner pays that means it's time to own the home you are living in. Home ownership comes with an amount of pride and joy. When you own your home you will take better care of it, therefore your neighborhood will look better and your property will value more in a short time, why not own the home you are living in?

There are several long- and short-term tax advantages that are associated with buying a home. If you itemize deductions, and you probably should, if you have a home mortgage, both the state and local taxes you pay on the property and the interest you pay on the mortgage, may be deductible from your adjusted gross income. Each dollar you pay in property taxes and interest saves you about 28 cents in federal income taxes. The higher your marginal tax rate, the greater the income tax rate will be. As a renter you cannot include these deductions in your income taxes. It is only the landlord that can deduct these as expenses.

The question of asking 'is it better to buy than to rent' should be clear in your mind by now. The intelligent decision would be to purchase your home, in fact there is everything to gain, and you will lose the opportunity of being a home owner.

If you can reflect on those numbers, we did in the previous paragraph you will see that it was a short-term calculation which was one year. Now our long- term calculation should be much better and shows a more profitable margin. The longer you own the property the more valuable it becomes to you!! The long term out- weigh the short- term. When you are purchasing your property, look on what it will do for you in a short period of time. If the short term looks good, then the long term will have a better outlook. This means that in the long run you will have more bread and butter as time progresses. If it looks good then it is good, so why wait.

Let us look on the family that is paying $1,000 each month for rent, what is the future of that family if they do not have a double income? It is just hard to say. They will end up paying, and paying, and paying. Look if they should remain at that apartment for 5 years you are looking at over $60,000 in rent because we are not sure of the type of increases that will take place over that period of time. Look at this, although you might consider yourself paying high rent, but let's say the landlord wants his apartment, he still has the option of giving you notice of termination, wouldn't he?

You might not like it, but what can you do about it, sooner or later you will have to go. You do not want this to happen, but in case it does happen, what will you have to take with you? $ 60,000 worth of rent receipts to go into the garbage.

Now look at this, the home is not yours and for the five years you contributed over $60,000, while the owner contributed under $35,000, isn't that enough reason why you should own your home? He pays less and gets the opportunity to stay and reap the benefit. Be the owner and pay less.

Making decisions can be a very complex process, but to decide whether to rent or to purchase should not be difficult. It is simple as making that decision as to whether you are ready, willing and able to take that first step to making that investment of your life time. Purchasing that home has to be a desire that has to be satisfactory which is to own the roof over your head. While you evaluate the outcome of your alternative, whatever you do, you have to make the right decision.

When you purchase a home, you are undertaking a sizable investment of your own money. I think that is where the question of should I rent or buy comes in. Much of your answers will depend upon expected future housing. When I speak of expected future housing, I am referring to you purchasing a home to live, or you are purchasing as an investor. It is your first home and you might not be sure of how you want to enter the real estate arena. You probably want to get the feel of what it is like before you make a decision of being an investor, or you might just want to play it safe and be a home owner. I would not attempt to tell you what to do once you are in the field, the end result will determine where you go from there.

ABOUT YOUR HOME

When you purchase your home, you want to be sure it is safely yours, but you will not know unless you do the things you are supposed to do. Even when you try to do all the things you thought were right, there are still the possibilities of making errors, although no room was given for errors. I remember closing on a property, a diligent search of the public record was done and failed to disclose a number of title defects, in spite of the search, nothing was revealed, nevertheless I went ahead and took a title insurance policy at closing in case any thing happened. It is not good to take certain chances with your investment, if you take care of your investment, it will in turn take care of you. I was at the closing when my attorney suggested I take title insurance because things do happen sometimes. I went ahead and took the coverage suggested, which was $90 for one year. Surprisingly, after 3 months I got a bill for $35,000 that was not shown on the title report. I referred the amount of the $35,000 to the title company, and they took care of it. Had it not been for that $90 insurance I would have ended up with a $35,000 bill. I have learned not to take certain chance; you have to know what chance to take and what not to.

The home, you purchase represent stability, performance and the hope for the future. Don't take chance with your home if you do, you may lose it, and if you lose it, chances are you may never replace it, so it makes, sense that for a small cost it does make good sense to protect yourself with title insurance. There are many companies out there, if you ask your attorney about title insurance, they will direct you to a pool of companies, you can pick one, or you may look up in your phone directory as they are listed there. Best wishes on your purchase. Do not leave yourself open to chance, be careful in your investments.

HINTS ON CALCULATING YOUR MORTGAGE

I have included some hints on how to calculate your mortgage when you are ready to shop for your home. I made them accessible so you will be able to familiarize yourself with the different tables. The chart that I have provided is simple and easy to be used. Don't be afraid, just find your mortgage amount and follow that amount across to the number of years you are taking your mortgage for and you can do your calculations. This could give you a first look even before you see your lender. It does not matter what bank or lending institution; the numbers will be the same. If your rate is 7%, it is just seven and will not change because of the type of institution. It is all good and well when you start shopping; you shop as a well-informed buyer. The more informed you are the more you will enjoy shopping for your new home. I believe that knowledge is power and that is why I'm giving you the relevant information necessary for buying your home. What you need to know is, when you calculate from the amortization sheet it will only give you the actual payment of the amount of money borrowed from the bank. This calculation does not have property tax, neither does it include the insurance; you need to find out those from the appropriate parties, your realtor will help you with that. When you get the estimate of your tax and insurance you may divide those numbers by twelve and then add them to the mortgage amount and that will give you your true monthly payment. The numbers might vary depending on where you are in the country; each state has their different laws and tax rates. Call up an insurance company, give them the price of the home and they will quote you a number, if they give you $ 1000 divide that number by twelve, which would be $83.00 to your mortgage plus taxes and that will give you your true monthly payment.

Except to where and when you would be required to pay Private Mortgage Insurance (PMI) on your mortgage that is below 2 0 percent down. It applies to the purchaser that is purchasing a home and the down payment is less than 20 percent. We call that 0 LTV need no PMI. 90 LTV would need PMI. Any mortgage 8 that is over 80 LTV has to have a Private Mortgage Insurance. There are some terms that you will not understand, what you need to do is to use your Dictionary to help give some of the clarification that you will need. I know everything would not be clear as you read, especially if you are reading this for the first time. Be smart, whatever you are not clear on, underlined those areas, or use a marker for highlighting. Remember the key word or words, whenever you are speaking with someone, find ways to interject the word or words you want clarifications for, and you will get your answer.

MONTHLY PAYMENT
NECESSARY TO AMORTIZE A LOAN

AMOUNT	1 YEAR	2 YEARS	3 YEARS	4 YEARS	5 YEARS	7 YEARS	8 YEARS	10 YEARS	12 YEARS
50	4 33	2 24	1 55	1 20	1 00	76	69	58	52
100	8 66	4 48	3 09	2 40	1 99	1 51	1 37	1 17	1 03
200	17 31	8 96	6 18	4 79	3 97	3 02	2 73	2 33	2 06
300	25 96	13 44	9 27	7 19	5 95	4 53	4 10	3 49	3 09
400	34 62	17 91	12 36	9 58	7 93	6 04	5 46	4 65	4 12
500	43 27	22 39	15 44	11 98	9 91	7 55	6 82	5 81	5 15
600	51 92	26 87	18 53	14 37	11 49	9 06	8 19	6 97	6 18
700	60 57	31 35	21 62	16 77	13 87	10 57	9 55	8 13	7 20
800	69 23	35 82	24 71	19 16	15 85	12 08	10 91	9 29	8 23
900	77 88	40 30	27 79	21 56	17 83	13 59	12 28	10 45	9 26
1000	86 53	44 78	30 88	23 95	19 81	15 10	13 64	11 62	10 29
2000	173 06	89 55	61 76	47 90	39 61	30 19	27 27	23 23	20 57
3000	259 59	134 32	92 64	71 84	59 41	45 28	40 91	34 84	30 86
4000	346 11	179 10	123 51	95 79	79 21	60 38	54 54	46 45	41 14
5000	432 64	223 87	154 39	119 74	99 01	75 47	68 17	58 06	51 42
6000	519 17	268 64	185 27	143 68	118 81	90 56	81 81	69 67	61 71
7000	605 69	313 41	216 14	167 63	138 61	105 65	95 44	81 28	71 99
8000	692 22	358 18	247 02	191 57	158 41	120 75	109 07	92 89	82 28
9000	778 75	402 96	277 90	215 52	178 22	135 84	122 71	104 50	92 56
10000	865 27	447 73	308 78	239 47	198 02	150 93	136 34	116 11	102 84
15000	1297 91	671 59	463 16	359 20	297 02	226 40	204 51	174 17	154 26
20000	1730 54	895 46	617 55	478 93	396 03	301 86	272 68	232 22	205 68
25000	2163 17	1119 32	771 93	598 66	495 03	377 32	340 85	290 28	257 10
30000	2595 81	1343 18	926 32	718 39	594 04	452 79	409 02	348 33	308 52
35000	3028 44	1567 05	1080 70	838 12	693 05	528 25	477 19	406 38	359 94
40000	3461 07	1790 91	1235 09	957 85	792 05	603 71	545 35	464 44	411 36
45000	3893 71	2014 77	1389 47	1077 59	891 06	679 18	613 52	522 49	462 78
46000	3980 24	2059 54	1420 35	1101 53	910 86	694 27	627 16	534 10	473 06
47000	4066 76	2104 32	1451 23	1125 48	930 66	709 36	640 79	545 71	483 34
48000	4153 29	2149 09	1482 11	1149 42	950 46	724 45	654 42	557 33	493 63
49000	4239 82	2193 86	1512 98	1173 37	970 26	739 55	668 06	568 94	503 91
50000	4326 34	2238 63	1543 86	1197 32	990 06	754 64	681 69	580 55	514 20
51000	4412 87	2283 41	1574 74	1221 26	1009 87	769 73	695 32	592 16	524 48
52000	4499 40	2328 18	1605 61	1245 21	1029 67	784 82	708 96	603 77	534 76
53000	4585 92	2372 95	1636 49	1269 16	1049 47	799 92	722 59	615 38	545 05
54000	4672 45	2417 72	1667 37	1293 10	1069 27	815 01	736 23	626 99	555 33
55000	4758 98	2462 50	1698 25	1317 05	1089 07	830 10	749 86	638 60	565 61
56000	4845 50	2507 27	1729 12	1340 99	1108 87	845 20	763 49	650 21	575 90
57000	4932 03	2552 04	1760 00	1364 94	1128 67	860 29	777 13	661 82	586 18
58000	5018 56	2596 81	1790 88	1388 89	1148 47	875 38	790 76	673 43	596 47
59000	5105 08	2641 59	1821 75	1412 83	1168 28	890 47	804 39	685 05	606 75
60000	5191 61	2686 36	1852 63	1436 78	1188 08	905 57	818 03	696 66	617 03
61000	5278 14	2731 13	1883 51	1460 73	1207 88	920 66	831 66	708 27	627 32
62000	5364 66	2775 90	1914 39	1484 67	1227 68	935 75	845 30	719 88	637 60
63000	5451 19	2820 68	1945 26	1508 62	1247 48	950 84	858 93	731 49	647 89
64000	5537 72	2865 45	1976 14	1532 56	1267 28	965 94	872 56	743 10	658 17
65000	5624 24	2910 22	2007 02	1556 51	1287 08	981 03	886 20	754 71	668 45
67500	5840 56	3022 15	2084 21	1616 38	1336 59	1018 76	920 28	783 74	694 16
70000	6056 88	3134 09	2161 40	1676 24	1386 09	1056 49	954 37	812 76	719 87
75000	6489 51	3357 95	2315 79	1795 97	1485 09	1131 96	1022 53	870 82	771 29
80000	6922 14	3581 81	2470 17	1915 70	1584 10	1207 42	1090 70	928 87	822 71
85000	7354 78	3805 67	2624 56	2035 44	1683 11	1282 88	1158 87	986 93	874 13
90000	7787 41	4029 54	2778 94	2155 17	1782 11	1358 35	1227 04	1044 98	925 55
95000	8220 05	4253 40	2933 33	2274 90	1881 12	1433 81	1295 21	1103 04	976 97
100000	8652 68	4477 26	3087 71	2394 63	1980 12	1509 27	1363 38	1161 09	1028 39
105000	9085 31	4701 13	3242 10	2514 36	2079 13	1584 74	1431 55	1219 14	1079 81
110000	9517 95	4924 99	3396 49	2634 09	2178 14	1660 20	1499 71	1277 20	1131 22
115000	9950 58	5148 85	3550 87	2753 82	2277 14	1735 66	1567 88	1335 25	1182 64
120000	10383 21	5372 71	3705 26	2873 55	2376 15	1811 13	1636 05	1393 31	1234 06
125000	10815 85	5596 58	3859 64	2993 29	2475 15	1886 59	1704 22	1451 36	1285 48
130000	11248 48	5820 44	4014 03	3113 02	2574 16	1962 05	1772 39	1509 42	1336 90
135000	11681 12	6044 30	4168 41	3232 75	2673 17	2037 52	1840 56	1567 47	1388 32
140000	12113 75	6268 17	4322 80	3352 48	2772 17	2112 98	1908 73	1625 52	1439 74
145000	12546 38	6492 03	4477 18	3472 21	2871 18	2188 44	1976 89	1683 58	1491 16
150000	12979 02	6715 89	4631 57	3591 94	2970 18	2263 91	2045 06	1741 63	1542 58

MONTHLY PAYMENT

NECESSARY TO AMORTIZE A LOAN

7%

AMOUNT	15 YEARS	18 YEARS	20 YEARS	25 YEARS	28 YEARS	29 YEARS	30 YEARS	35 YEARS	40 YEARS
50	.45	.41	.39	.36	.34	.34	.34	.32	.32
100	.90	.82	.78	.71	.68	.68	.67	.64	.63
200	1.80	1.64	1.56	1.42	1.36	1.35	1.34	1.28	1.25
300	2.70	2.45	2.33	2.13	2.04	2.02	2.00	1.92	1.89
400	3.60	3.27	3.11	2.83	2.72	2.69	2.67	2.56	2.49
500	4.50	4.08	3.88	3.54	3.40	3.37	3.33	3.20	3.11
600	5.40	4.90	4.66	4.25	4.08	4.04	4.00	3.84	3.73
700	6.30	5.71	5.43	4.95	4.76	4.71	4.66	4.48	4.36
800	7.20	6.53	6.21	5.66	5.44	5.38	5.33	5.12	4.98
900	8.09	7.34	6.98	6.37	6.12	6.05	5.99	5.75	5.60
1000	8.99	8.16	7.76	7.07	6.80	6.73	6.66	6.39	6.22
2000	17.98	16.32	15.51	14.14	13.60	13.45	13.31	12.78	12.43
3000	26.97	24.47	23.26	21.21	20.39	20.17	19.96	19.17	18.65
4000	35.96	32.63	31.02	28.28	27.19	26.88	26.63	25.56	24.86
5000	44.95	40.79	38.77	35.34	33.99	33.61	33.27	31.95	31.08
6000	53.93	48.94	46.52	42.41	40.78	40.33	39.92	38.34	37.29
7000	62.92	57.09	54.28	49.48	47.58	47.05	46.58	44.72	43.51
8000	71.91	65.25	62.03	56.55	54.37	53.78	53.23	51.11	49.72
9000	80.90	73.40	69.78	63.62	61.17	60.50	59.88	57.50	55.93
10000	89.89	81.56	77.53	70.69	67.97	67.22	66.54	63.89	62.15
15000	134.83	122.33	116.30	106.02	101.95	100.82	99.80	95.83	93.22
20000	179.77	163.11	155.06	141.36	135.93	134.43	133.07	127.78	124.29
25000	224.71	203.88	193.83	176.70	169.91	168.04	166.33	159.72	155.36
30000	269.65	244.66	232.59	212.04	203.89	201.64	199.60	191.66	186.43
35000	314.59	285.43	271.36	247.38	237.87	235.25	232.88	223.60	217.51
40000	359.54	326.21	310.12	282.72	271.85	268.86	266.13	255.55	248.58
45000	404.48	366.98	348.83	318.06	305.83	302.46	299.39	287.49	279.65
46000	413.47	375.14	356.64	325.12	312.62	309.18	306.04	293.88	285.86
47000	422.45	383.29	364.40	332.19	319.42	315.91	312.70	300.27	292.08
48000	431.44	391.45	372.15	339.26	326.22	322.63	319.35	306.66	298.29
49000	440.43	399.60	379.90	346.33	333.01	329.35	326.00	313.04	304.51
50000	449.42	407.78	387.65	353.39	339.81	336.07	332.66	319.43	310.72
51000	458.41	415.91	395.41	360.46	346.61	342.79	339.32	325.82	316.93
52000	467.40	424.07	403.16	367.53	353.40	349.51	345.96	332.21	323.15
53000	476.38	432.22	410.91	374.60	360.20	356.23	352.62	338.60	329.36
54000	485.37	440.38	418.67	381.67	366.99	362.96	359.27	344.99	335.58
55000	494.36	448.53	426.42	388.73	373.78	369.68	365.92	351.38	341.78
56000	503.35	456.69	434.17	395.80	380.59	376.40	372.57	357.76	348.01
57000	512.34	464.84	441.93	402.87	387.38	383.12	379.23	364.15	354.22
58000	521.33	473.00	448.68	409.94	394.18	389.84	385.88	370.54	360.44
59000	530.31	481.15	457.43	417.00	400.97	398.58	392.53	376.93	366.65
60000	539.30	489.31	465.18	424.07	407.77	403.28	399.18	383.32	372.88
61000	548.29	497.46	472.94	431.14	414.57	410.00	405.84	389.71	379.08
62000	557.28	505.62	480.69	438.21	421.36	416.73	412.49	396.10	385.29
63000	566.27	513.77	488.44	445.28	428.16	423.45	419.15	402.48	391.51
64000	575.26	521.93	496.20	452.34	434.95	430.17	425.80	408.87	397.72
65000	584.24	530.08	503.95	459.41	441.75	436.89	432.45	415.26	403.94
67500	606.71	550.47	523.33	477.08	458.74	453.69	449.08	431.23	419.47
70000	629.18	570.86	542.71	494.75	475.73	470.50	465.78	447.20	435.01
75000	674.13	611.63	581.48	530.09	509.71	504.10	498.85	479.15	466.08
80000	719.07	652.41	620.24	565.43	543.69	537.71	532.28	511.09	497.15
85000	764.01	693.18	659.01	600.77	577.67	571.32	565.91	543.03	528.22
90000	808.95	733.96	697.77	636.11	611.65	604.92	598.78	574.98	559.29
95000	853.89	774.73	736.54	671.45	645.63	638.53	632.04	606.92	590.36
100000	898.82	815.51	775.30	706.78	679.61	672.14	665.31	638.86	621.44
105000	943.77	856.28	814.07	742.12	713.58	705.74	698.57	670.80	652.51
110000	988.72	897.06	852.83	777.46	747.57	739.35	731.84	702.75	683.58
115000	1033.66	937.83	891.60	812.80	781.55	772.95	765.10	734.69	714.65
120000	1078.60	978.61	930.36	848.14	815.54	806.56	798.37	766.63	745.72
125000	1123.54	1019.38	969.13	883.48	849.52	840.17	831.63	798.58	776.79
130000	1188.48	1060.16	1007.89	918.82	883.50	873.77	864.90	830.52	807.87
135000	1213.42	1100.93	1046.66	954.16	917.48	907.38	898.16	862.46	838.94
140000	1258.36	1141.71	1085.42	989.50	951.46	940.99	931.43	894.40	870.01
145000	1303.31	1182.48	1124.19	1024.83	985.44	974.59	964.69	926.35	901.08
150000	1348.25	1223.26	1162.95	1060.17	1019.42	1008.20	997.96	958.29	932.15

7⅛% MONTHLY PAYMENT
NECESSARY TO AMORTIZE A LOAN

AMOUNT	1 YEAR	2 YEARS	3 YEARS	4 YEARS	5 YEARS	7 YEARS	8 YEARS	10 YEARS	12 YEARS
50	4.33	2.25	1.55	1.21	1.00	.78	.69	.59	.52
100	8.66	4.49	3.10	2.41	1.99	1.52	1.37	1.17	1.04
200	17.32	8.97	6.19	4.81	3.98	3.04	2.74	2.34	2.08
300	25.98	13.45	9.29	7.21	5.96	4.55	4.11	3.51	3.11
400	34.64	17.94	12.38	9.61	7.95	6.07	5.48	4.68	4.15
500	43.30	22.42	15.47	12.01	9.94	7.58	6.85		5.18
600	51.96	26.90	18.57	14.41	11.92	9.10	8.22		6.22
700	60.61	31.39	21.66	18.81	13.91	10.61	9.59	• . •	7.25
800	69.27	35.87	24.75	19.21	15.89	12.13	10.96	9.35	8.29
900	77.93	40.35	27.85	21.61	17.88	13.64	12.33	10.51	9.32
1000	86.59	44.83	30.94	24.01	19.87	15.16	13.70	11.68	10.36
2000	173.17	89.66	61.87	48.01	39.73	30.31	27.40	23.36	20.71
3000	259.76	134.49	92.81	72.02	59.59	45.47	41.09	35.03	31.06
4000	346.34	179.32	123.74	96.02	79.45	60.62	54.79	46.71	41.41
5000	432.93	224.15	154.68	120.03	99.31	75.77	68.49	58.39	51.76
6000	519.51	268.98	185.61	144.03	119.17	90.93	82.18	70.06	62.11
7000	606.10	313.81	216.54	168.03	139.03	106.08	95.88	81.73	72.46
8000	692.68	358.64	247.48	192.04	158.89	121.24	109.57	93.41	82.81
9000	770.26	403.47	278.41	216.04	178.75	136.39	123.27	105.08	93.16
10000	865.85	448.30	309.35	240.05	198.61	151.54	136.97	116.76	103.51
15000	1298.77	672.44	464.02	360.07	297.91	227.31	205.45	175.14	155.26
20000	1731.69	896.59	618.69	480.09	397.21	303.08	273.93	233.51	207.02
25000	2164.61	1120.74	773.36	600.11	496.51	378.85	342.41	291.89	258.77
30000	2597.54	1344.88	928.03	720.13	595.81	454.62	410.89	350.27	310.52
35000	3030.46	1569.03	1082.70	840.15	695.11	530.39	479.37	408.64	362.27
40000	3463.38	1793.18	1237.38	960.18	794.41	606.16	547.85	467.02	414.03
45000	3896.30	2017.32	1392.05	1080.20	893.72	681.93	616.33	525.40	465.78
46000	3982.89	2062.15	1422.98	1104.20	913.58	697.08	630.02	537.07	476.13
47000	4069.47	2106.98	1453.92	1128.21	933.44	712.24	643.72	548.75	486.48
48000	4156.06	2151.81	1484.85	1152.21	953.30	727.39	657.41	560.42	496.83
49000	4242.64	2186.64	1515.78	1176.21	973.16	742.54	671.11	572.10	507.18
50000	4329.22	2241.47	1546.72	1200.22	993.02	757.70	684.81	583.77	517.53
51000	4415.81	2288.30	1577.65	1224.22	1012.88	772.85	698.50	595.45	527.88
52000	4502.39	2331.13	1608.59	1248.23	1032.74	788.01	712.20	607.12	538.23
53000	4588.98	2375.96	1639.52	1272.23	1052.60	803.16	725.89	618.80	548.58
54000	4675.56	2420.79	1670.46	1296.24	1072.46	818.31	739.59	630.48	558.94
55000	4762.15	2465.61	1701.39	1320.24	1092.32	833.47	753.28	642.15	569.29
56000	4848.73	2510.44	1732.32	1344.24	1112.18	848.62	766.98	653.83	579.64
57000	4935.31	2555.27	1763.26	1368.25	1132.04	863.77	780.68	665.50	589.99
58000	5021.90	2600.10	1794.19	1392.25	1151.90	878.93	794.37	677.18	600.34
59000	5108.48	2644.93	1825.13	1416.26	1171.76	894.08	808.07	688.85	610.69
60000	5195.07	2689.76	1856.06	1440.26	1191.62	909.24	821.77	700.53	621.04
61000	5281.65	2734.59	1887.00	1464.27	1211.48	924.39	835.46	712.20	631.39
62000	5368.24	2779.42	1917.93	1488.27	1231.34	939.54	849.16	723.88	641.74
63000	5454.82	2824.25	1948.86	1512.27	1251.20	954.70	862.85	735.55	652.09
64000	5541.41	2869.08	1979.80	1536.28	1271.06	969.85	876.55	747.23	662.44
65000	5627.99	2913.91	2010.73	1560.28	1290.92	985.01	890.25	758.90	672.79
67500	5844.45	3025.98	2088.07	1620.29	1340.57	1022.89	924.49	788.09	698.67
70000	6060.91	3138.05	2165.40	1680.30	1390.22	1060.78	958.73	817.28	724.54
75000	6493.83	3362.20	2320.08	1800.33	1489.52	1136.54	1027.21	875.66	776.30
80000	6926.76	3586.35	2474.75	1920.35	1588.82	1212.31	1095.69	934.03	828.05
85000	7359.68	3810.49	2629.42	2040.37	1688.12	1288.08	1164.17	992.41	879.80
90000	7792.60	4034.64	2784.09	2160.39	1787.43	1363.85	1232.65	1050.79	931.56
95000	8225.52	4258.79	2938.76	2280.41	1886.73	1439.62	1301.13	1109.17	983.31
100000	8658.44	4482.93	3093.43	2400.43	1986.03	1515.39	1369.61	1167.54	1035.06
105000	9091.37	4707.08	3248.10	2520.45	2085.33	1591.16	1438.09	1225.92	1086.81
110000	9524.29	4931.22	3402.78	2640.45	2184.63	1666.93	1506.57	1284.30	1138.57
115000	9957.21	5155.37	3557.45	2760.50	2283.93	1742.70	1575.05	1342.67	1190.32
120000	10390.13	5379.52	3712.12	2880.52	2383.23	1818.47	1643.53	1401.05	1242.07
125000	10823.05	5603.66	3866.79	3000.54	2482.53	1894.24	1712.01	1459.43	1293.83
130000	11255.97	5827.81	4021.46	3120.56	2581.83	1970.01	1780.49	1517.80	1345.58
135000	11688.90	6051.96	4176.13	3240.58	2681.14	2045.78	1848.97	1576.18	1397.33
140000	12121.82	6276.10	4330.80	3360.60	2780.44	2121.55	1917.45	1634.56	1449.08
145000	12554.74	6500.25	4485.48	3480.63	2879.74	2197.31	1985.93	1692.93	1500.84
150000	12987.66	6724.40	4640.15	3600.65	2979.04	2273.08	2054.41	1751.31	1552.59

MONTHLY PAYMENT 7⅛%
NECESSARY TO AMORTIZE A LOAN

AMOUNT	15 YEARS	18 YEARS	20 YEARS	25 YEARS	28 YEARS	29 YEARS	30 YEARS	35 YEARS	40 YEARS
50	46	42	40	36	35	35	34	33	32
100	91	83	79	72	69	69	68	65	64
200	182	165	157	143	138	137	135	130	127
300	272	247	235	215	207	205	203	195	190
400	363	330	314	286	276	273	270	260	253
500	453	412	392	358	344	341	337	324	316
600	544	494	470	429	413	409	405	389	379
700	635	576	548	501	482	477	472	454	442
800	725	659	627	572	551	545	539	519	505
900	816	741	705	644	620	613	607	583	568
1000	906	823	783	715	688	681	674	648	631
2000	1812	1648	1566	1430	1376	1361	1348	1296	1262
3000	2718	2469	2349	2145	2064	2042	2022	1943	1892
4000	3624	3292	3132	2860	2752	2722	2695	2591	2523
5000	4530	4115	3915	3574	3440	3403	3369	3239	3153
6000	5435	4937	4697	4289	4128	4083	4043	3886	3784
7000	6341	5760	5480	5004	4816	4764	4717	4534	4414
8000	7247	6583	6263	5719	5503	5444	5390	5182	5045
9000	8153	7406	7046	6433	6191	6125	6064	5829	5675
10000	9059	8229	7829	7148	6879	6805	6738	6477	6306
15000	13588	12343	11743	10722	10318	10207	10106	9715	9458
20000	18117	16457	15657	14296	13758	13610	13475	12953	12611
25000	22646	20571	19571	17870	17197	17012	16843	16192	15764
30000	27175	24685	23485	21444	20636	20414	20212	19430	18916
35000	31705	28799	27399	25018	24075	23817	23581	22668	22069
40000	36234	32913	31313	28591	27515	27219	26949	25906	25222
45000	40763	37027	35227	32165	30954	30621	30318	29144	28374
46000	41669	37850	36010	32680	31642	31302	30992	29792	29005
47000	42575	38673	36793	33595	32330	31982	31665	30440	29635
48000	43480	39496	37576	34310	33018	32663	32339	31087	30266
49000	44385	40319	38359	35024	33706	33343	33013	31735	30897
50000	45292	41142	39141	35739	34394	34024	33686	32383	31527
51000	46195	41954	39924	36454	35081	34704	34360	33030	32158
52000	47104	42787	40707	37169	35769	35385	35034	33678	32788
53000	48010	43610	41490	37883	36457	36065	35708	34325	33419
54000	48915	44433	42273	38598	37145	36748	36381	34973	34049
55000	49821	45256	43056	39313	37833	37426	37055	35621	34680
56000	50727	46078	43838	40028	38521	38107	37729	36268	35310
57000	51633	46901	44621	40743	39209	38787	38402	36918	35941
58000	52539	47724	45404	41457	39897	39468	39076	37564	36571
59000	53445	48547	46187	42172	40584	40148	39750	38211	37202
60000	54350	49370	46970	42887	41272	40828	40424	38859	37832
61000	55256	50193	47753	43602	41960	41509	41097	39507	38463
62000	56162	51015	48535	44318	42648	42189	41771	40154	39093
63000	57068	51838	49318	45031	43336	42870	42445	40802	39724
64000	57974	52661	50101	45748	44024	43550	43118	41450	40355
65000	58880	53484	50884	46461	44712	44231	43792	42097	40985
67500	61144	55541	52841	48249	46431	45932	45477	43718	42581
70000	63409	57598	54798	50035	48151	47633	47161	45335	44138
75000	67938	61712	58712	53608	51590	51035	50528	48574	47290
80000	72467	65826	62626	57182	55029	54438	53898	51812	50443
85000	76996	69940	66540	60756	58469	57767	57267	55050	53596
90000	81525	74054	70454	64330	61908	61242	60636	58288	56749
95000	86054	78168	74368	67904	65347	64645	64004	61526	59901
100000	90584	82283	78282	71478	68787	68047	67372	64765	63054
105000	95113	86397	82197	75052	72226	71449	70741	68003	66206
110000	99642	90511	86111	78626	75665	74852	74110	71241	69359
115000	104171	94625	90025	82199	79105	78254	77478	74479	72512
120000	108700	98739	93939	85773	82544	81656	80847	77717	75664
125000	113229	102853	97853	89347	85983	85059	84215	80956	78817
130000	117759	106967	101767	92921	89423	88461	87584	84194	81970
135000	122288	111081	105681	96495	92862	91863	90953	87432	85122
140000	126817	115195	109595	100069	96301	95266	94321	90670	88275
145000	131346	119310	113509	103643	99741	98668	97690	93908	91428
150000	135875	123424	117423	107216	103180	102070	101058	97147	94580

7 ¼ % MONTHLY PAYMENT
NECESSARY TO AMORTIZE A LOAN

AMOUNT	1 YEAR	2 YEARS	3 YEARS	4 YEARS	5 YEARS	7 YEARS	8 YEARS	10 YEARS	12 YEARS
50	4.34	2.25	1.55	1.21	1.00	77	69	59	53
100	8.67	4.49	3.10	2.41	2.00	1.53	1.38	1.19	1.05
200	17.33	8.98	6.20	4.82	3.99	3.05	2.76	2.35	2.09
300	26.00	13.47	9.30	7.22	5.98	4.57	4.13	3.53	3.13
400	34.66	17.96	12.40	9.63	7.97	6.09	5.51	4.70	4.17
500	43.33	22.45	15.50	12.04	9.96	7.61	6.88	5.88	5.21
600	51.99	26.94	18.60	14.44	11.96	9.13	8.26	7.05	6.26
700	60.65	31.43	21.70	16.85	13.95	10.66	9.64	8.22	7.30
800	69.32	35.91	24.80	19.25	15.94	12.18	11.01	9.40	8.34
900	77.98	40.40	27.90	21.66	17.93	13.70	12.39	10.57	9.38
1000	86.65	44.89	31.00	24.07	19.92	15.22	13.78	11.75	10.42
2000	173.29	89.78	61.99	48.13	39.84	30.44	27.52	23.49	20.84
3000	259.93	134.66	92.98	72.19	59.76	45.65	41.28	35.23	31.26
4000	346.57	179.55	123.97	96.25	79.68	60.87	55.04	46.97	41.68
5000	433.22	224.44	154.96	120.32	99.60	76.08	68.80	58.71	52.09
6000	519.86	269.32	185.95	144.38	119.52	91.30	82.56	70.45	62.51
7000	606.50	314.21	216.93	168.44	139.44	106.51	96.31	82.19	72.93
8000	693.14	359.09	247.94	192.50	159.35	121.73	110.07	93.93	83.35
9000	779.78	403.98	278.93	216.57	179.28	136.94	123.83	105.67	93.76
10000	866.43	448.87	309.92	240.63	199.20	152.16	137.59	117.41	104.18
15000	1299.64	673.30	464.88	380.94	298.80	228.23	206.38	176.11 *	156.27
20000	1732.85	897.73	619.84	481.25	398.39	304.31	275.17	234.81 **	208.36
25000	2166.06	1122.16	774.79	601.57	497.99	380.38	343.97	293.51	260.44
30000	2599.27	1346.59	929.75	721.88	597.59	456.46	412.76	352.21	312.53
35000	3032.48	1571.02	1084.71	842.19	697.18	532.54	481.55	410.91	364.62
40000	3465.69	1795.45	1239.67	962.50	796.78	608.61	550.34	469.61	416.71
45000	3898.90	2019.88	1394.62	1082.81	896.38	684.69	619.14	528.31	468.80
46000	3985.54	2064.76	1425.62	1106.88	916.30	699.90	632.89	540.05	479.21
47000	4072.18	2109.65	1456.61	1130.94	936.21	715.12	646.65	551.79	489.63
48000	4158.82	2154.53	1487.60	1155.00	956.13	730.33	660.41	563.53	500.05
49000	4245.46	2199.42	1518.59	1179.06	976.05	745.55	674.17	575.27	510.47
50000	4332.11	2244.31	1549.58	1203.13	995.97	760.76	687.93	587.01	520.88
51000	4418.75	2289.19	1580.57	1227.19	1015.89	775.98	701.69	598.75	531.30
52000	4505.39	2334.08	1611.56	1251.25	1035.81	791.19	715.44	610.49	541.72
53000	4592.03	2378.96	1642.56	1275.31	1055.73	806.41	729.20	622.23	552.14
54000	4678.68	2423.85	1673.55	1299.37	1075.65	821.62	742.96	633.97	562.55
55000	4765.32	2468.74	1704.54	1323.44	1095.57	836.84	756.72	645.71	572.97
56000	4851.96	2513.62	1735.53	1347.50	1115.49	852.06	770.48	657.45	583.39
57000	4938.60	2558.51	1766.52	1371.56	1135.41	867.27	784.24	669.19	593.81
58000	5025.24	2603.39	1797.51	1395.62	1155.33	882.49	798.00	680.93	604.22
59000	5111.89	2648.28	1828.51	1419.69	1175.25	897.70	811.75	692.67	614.64
60000	5198.53	2693.17	1859.50	1443.75	1195.17	912.92	825.51	704.41	625.06
61000	5285.17	2738.05	1890.49	1467.81	1215.09	928.13	839.27	716.15	635.48
62000	5371.81	2782.94	1921.48	1491.87	1235.01	943.35	853.03	727.89	645.89
63000	5458.45	2827.82	1952.47	1515.94	1254.92	958.56	866.79	739.63	656.31
64000	5545.10	2872.71	1983.46	1540.00	1274.84	973.78	880.55	751.37	666.73
65000	5631.74	2917.60	2014.45	1564.06	1294.76	988.99	894.30	763.11	677.15
67000	5848.34	3029.81	2091.93	1624.22	1344.56	1027.03	928.70	792.46	703.19
70000	6064.95	3142.03	2169.41	1684.37	1394.36	1065.07	963.10	821.81	729.23
75000	6498.18	3366.48	2324.37	1804.69	1493.96	1141.14	1031.89	880.51	781.32
80000	6931.37	3590.88	2479.33	1925.00	1593.55	1217.22	1100.68	939.21	833.41
85000	7364.58	3815.32	2634.28	2045.31	1693.15	1293.30	1169.47	997.91	885.50
90000	7797.79	4039.75	2789.24	2165.62	1792.75	1369.37	1238.27	1056.61	937.59
95000	8231.00	4264.18	2944.20	2285.93	1892.34	1445.45	1307.06	1115.31	989.67
100000	8664.21	4488.61	3099.16	2406.25	1991.94	1521.52	1375.85	1174.02	1041.76
105000	9097.42	4713.04	3254.12	2526.56	2091.54	1597.60	1444.64	1232.72	1093.85
110000	9530.63	4937.47	3409.07	2646.87	2191.13	1673.68	1513.44	1291.42	1145.94
115000	9963.84	5161.90	3564.03	2767.18	2290.73	1749.75	1582.23	1350.12	1198.03
120000	10397.05	5386.33	3718.99	2887.49	2390.33	1825.83	1651.02	1408.82	1250.11
125000	10830.26	5610.76	3873.95	3007.81	2489.93	1901.90	1719.81	1467.52	1302.20
130000	11263.47	5835.19	4028.90	3128.12	2589.52	1977.98	1788.60	1526.22	1354.29
135000	11696.68	6059.62	4183.86	3248.43	2689.12	2054.05	1857.40	1584.92	1406.38
140000	12129.88	6284.05	4338.82	3368.74	2788.72	2130.13	1926.19	1643.62	1458.46
145000	12563.10	6508.48	4493.78	3489.05	2888.31	2206.21	1994.98	1702.32	1510.55
150000	12996.31	6732.91	4648.73	3609.37	2987.91	2282.28	2063.77	1761.02	1562.64

92

MONTHLY PAYMENT 7¼%

NECESSARY TO AMORTIZE A LOAN

AMOUNT	15 YEARS	18 YEARS	20 YEARS	25 YEARS	28 YEARS	29 YEARS	30 YEARS	35 YEARS	40 YEARS
50	46	42	40	37	35	35	35	33	32
100	92	84	80	73	70	69	69	66	64
200	183	167	159	145	140	138	137	132	128
300	274	250	238	217	209	207	206	197	192
400	366	333	317	290	278	276	273	263	256
500	457	416	396	362	349	345	342	329	320
600	548	499	475	434	418	414	410	394	384
700	640	582	554	506	488	483	478	460	448
800	731	665	633	579	557	552	546	526	512
900	822	748	712	651	627	620	614	591	576
1000	913	831	791	723	697	689	683	657	640
2000	1826	1661	1581	1446	1393	1378	1365	1313	1280
3000	2739	2491	2372	2169	2089	2067	2047	1970	1920
4000	3652	3321	3162	2892	2785	2756	2729	2626	2559
5000	4565	4151	3952	3615	3481	3445	3411	3283	3199
6000	5478	4982	4743	4337	4177	4134	4094	3939	3839
7000	6391	5812	5533	5060	4874	4822	4776	4596	4478
8000	7303	6642	6324	5783	5570	5511	5458	5252	5119
9000	8216	7472	7114	6506	6266	6200	6140	5909	5759
10000	9129	8302	7904	7229	6962	6889	6822	6565	6397
15000	13693	12453	11856	10843	10443	10333	10233	9848	9596
20000	18258	16604	15808	14457	13924	13777	13644	13130	12794
25000	22822	20755	19760	18071	17404	17222	17055	16412	15992
30000	27386	24906	23712	21685	20885	20666	20466	19695	19191
35000	31951	29057	27664	25299	24366	24110	23877	22977	22389
40000	36515	33207	31616	28913	27847	27554	27288	26259	25587
45000	41079	37358	35567	32527	31328	30998	30698	29542	28786
46000	41992	38188	36358	33230	32024	31687	31381	30198	29425
47000	42905	39019	37148	33972	32720	32376	32063	30854	30065
48000	43818	39849	37939	34695	33416	33065	32745	31511	30705
49000	44731	40679	38729	35418	34112	33754	33427	32167	31344
50000	45644	41509	39519	36141	34808	34443	34109	32824	31984
51000	46557	42339	40310	36864	35505	35132	34791	33480	32624
52000	47469	43169	41100	37586	36201	35820	35474	34137	33263
53000	48382	44000	41890	38309	36897	36509	36156	34793	33903
54000	49295	44830	42681	39032	37593	37198	36838	35450	34543
55000	50208	45660	43471	39755	38289	37887	37520	36106	35182
56000	51121	46490	44262	40478	38985	38576	38202	36763	35822
57000	52034	47320	45052	41200	39681	39265	38885	37419	36462
58000	52947	48150	45842	41923	40378	39953	39567	38076	37101
59000	53859	48981	46633	42646	41074	40642	40249	38732	37741
60000	54772	49811	47423	43369	41770	41331	40931	39389	38381
61000	55685	50641	48213	44092	42466	42020	41613	40045	39020
62000	56598	51471	49004	44815	43162	42709	42295	40701	39660
63000	57511	52301	49794	45537	43858	43398	42978	41358	40300
64000	58424	53132	50585	46260	44555	44086	43660	42014	40940
65000	59337	53962	51375	46983	45251	44775	44342	42671	41579
67500	61619	56037	53351	48790	46989	46497	46047	44312	43178
70000	63801	58113	55327	50597	48731	48220	47753	45953	44778
75000	68485	62263	59279	54211	52212	51664	51164	49236	47976
80000	73030	66414	63231	57825	55693	55108	54575	52518	51174
85000	77594	70565	67182	61439	59174	58552	57985	55800	54373
90000	82158	74716	71134	65053	62655	61996	61396	59083	57571
95000	86722	78867	75086	68667	66135	65441	64807	62365	60769
100000	91287	83018	79038	72281	69616	68885	68219	65647	63968
105000	95851	87169	82990	75895	73097	72329	71629	68930	67166
110000	100415	91319	86942	79509	76578	75773	75040	72212	70364
115000	104980	95470	90894	83123	80059	79217	78451	75494	73563
120000	109544	99621	94846	86737	83539	82662	81862	78777	76761
125000	114108	103772	98797	90351	87020	86106	85273	82059	79959
130000	118673	107923	102749	93965	90501	89550	88683	85341	83158
135000	123237	112074	106701	97579	93982	92994	92094	88624	86356
140000	127801	116225	110653	101193	97462	96439	95505	91908	89555
145000	132366	120375	114605	104807	100943	99883	98916	95188	92753
150000	136930	124526	118557	108422	104424	103327	102327	98471	95951

93

7⅜% MONTHLY PAYMENT
NECESSARY TO AMORTIZE A LOAN

AMOUNT	1 YEAR	2 YEARS	3 YEARS	4 YEARS	5 YEARS	7 YEARS	8 YEARS	10 YEARS	12 YEARS
50	4 34	2 25	1 56	1 21	1 00	77	70	60	53
100	8 67	4 50	3 11	2 42	2 00	1 53	1 39	1 19	1 05
200	17 34	8 99	6 21	4 83	4 00	3 06	2 77	2 37	2 10
300	26 01	13 49	9 32	7 24	6 00	4 59	4 15	3 55	3 15
400	34 68	17 98	12 42	9 65	8 00	6 12	5 53	4 73	4 20
500	43 35	22 48	15 53	12 07	9 99	7 64	6 92	5 91	5 25
600	52 02	26 97	18 63	14 48	11 99	9 17	8 30	7 09	6 30
700	60 69	31 46	21 74	16 89	13 99	10 70	9 68	8 27	7 34
800	69 36	35 96	24 84	19 30	15 99	12 23	11 06	9 45	8 39
900	78 03	40 45	27 95	21 71	17 99	13 75	12 44	10 63	9 44
1000	86 70	44 95	31 05	24 13	19 98	15 28	13 83	11 81	10 49
2000	173 40	89 89	62 10	48 25	39 96	30 56	27 65	23 62	20 97
3000	260 10	134 83	93 15	72 37	59 94	45 83	41 47	35 42	31 46
4000	346 80	179 78	124 20	96 49	79 92	61 11	55 29	47 23	41 94
5000	433 50	224 72	155 25	120 61	99 90	76 39	69 11	59 03	52 43
6000	520 20	269 66	186 30	144 73	119 88	91 66	82 93	70 84	62 91
7000	606 90	314 60	217 35	168 85	139 86	106 94	96 75	82 64	73 40
8000	693 60	359 55	248 40	192 97	159 83	122 22	110 57	94 45	83 88
9000	780 30	404 49	279 44	217 09	179 81	137 49	124 39	106 25	94 37
10000	867 00	449 43	310 49	241 21	199 79	152 77	138 22	118 06	104 85
15000	1300 50	674 15	465 74	361 81	299 68	229 15	207 32	177 08	157 28
20000	1734 00	898 86	620 98	482 42	399 58	305 54	276 43	236 11	209 70
25000	2167 50	1123 57	776 23	603 02	499 47	381 92	345 53	295 13	262 12
30000	2601 00	1348 29	931 47	723 62	599 36	458 30	414 64	354 16	314 55
35000	3034 50	1573 00	1086 71	844 23	699 26	534 69	483 74	413 18	366 97
40000	3467 99	1797 72	1241 96	964 83	799 15	611 07	552 85	472 21	419 40
45000	3901 49	2022 43	1397 20	1085 43	899 04	687 45	621 95	531 23	471 82
46000	3988 19	2067 37	1428 25	1109 55	919 02	702 73	635 77	543 04	482 31
47000	4074 89	2112 32	1459 30	1133 67	939 00	718 01	649 60	554 84	492 79
48000	4161 59	2157 26	1490 35	1157 79	958 98	733 28	663 42	566 65	503 27
49000	4248 29	2202 20	1521 40	1181 91	978 96	748 56	677 24	578 45	513 76
50000	4334 99	2247 14	1552 45	1206 04	998 94	763 84	691 06	590 26	524 24
51000	4421 69	2292 09	1583 50	1230 16	1018 91	779 11	704 88	602 06	534 73
52000	4508 39	2337 03	1614 54	1254 28	1038 89	794 39	718 70	613 87	545 21
53000	4595 09	2381 97	1645 59	1278 40	1058 87	809 67	732 52	625 67	555 70
54000	4681 79	2426 91	1676 64	1302 52	1078 85	824 94	746 34	637 48	566 18
55000	4768 49	2471 86	1707 69	1326 64	1098 83	840 22	760 16	649 28	576 67
56000	4855 19	2516 80	1738 74	1350 76	1118 81	855 50	773 99	661 09	587 15
57000	4941 89	2561 74	1769 79	1374 88	1138 79	870 77	787 81	672 89	597 64
58000	5028 59	2606 69	1800 84	1399 00	1158 76	886 05	801 63	684 70	608 12
59000	5115 29	2651 63	1831 89	1423 12	1178 74	901 33	815 45	696 50	618 61
60000	5201 99	2696 57	1862 94	1447 24	1198 72	916 60	829 27	708 31	629 09
61000	5288 69	2741 51	1893 98	1471 36	1218 70	931 88	843 09	720 11	639 58
62000	5375 39	2786 46	1925 03	1495 48	1238 68	947 16	856 91	731 92	650 06
63000	5462 09	2831 40	1956 08	1519 60	1258 66	962 43	870 73	743 72	660 55
64000	5548 79	2876 34	1987 13	1543 72	1278 64	977 71	884 55	755 53	671 03
65000	5635 49	2921 29	2018 18	1567 84	1298 61	992 99	898 38	767 33	681 52
87500	5852 24	3033 84	2095 80	1628 15	1348 56	1031 18	932 93	796 85	707 73
70000	6068 99	3146 00	2173 42	1688 45	1398 51	1069 37	967 48	826 38	733 94
75000	6502 48	3370 71	2328 67	1809 05	1498 40	1145 75	1036 58	885 38	786 36
80000	6935 98	3595 43	2483 91	1929 65	1598 29	1222 14	1105 69	944 41	838 79
85000	7369 48	3820 14	2639 16	2050 26	1698 19	1298 52	1174 80	1003 43	891 21
90000	7802 98	4044 85	2794 40	2170 86	1798 08	1374 90	1243 90	1062 46	943 64
95000	8236 48	4269 57	2949 64	2291 46	1897 97	1451 29	1313 01	1121 48	996 06
100000	8669 98	4494 28	3104 89	2412 07	1997 87	1527 67	1382 11	1180 51	1048 48
105000	9103 48	4719 00	3260 13	2532 67	2097 76	1604 05	1451 22	1239 53	1100 91
110000	9536 97	4943 71	3415 38	2653 27	2197 65	1680 44	1520 32	1298 56	1153 33
115000	9970 47	5168 42	3570 62	2773 88	2297 54	1756 82	1589 43	1357 58	1205 76
120000	10403 97	5393 14	3725 87	2894 48	2397 44	1833 20	1658 53	1416 61	1258 18
125000	10837 47	5617 85	3881 11	3015 08	2497 33	1909 59	1727 64	1475 63	1310 60
130000	11270 97	5842 57	4036 35	3135 68	2597 22	1985 97	1796 75	1534 66	1363 03
135000	11704 47	6067 28	4191 60	3256 29	2697 12	2062 35	1865 85	1593 69	1415 45
140000	12137 97	6291 99	4346 84	3376 89	2797 01	2138 74	1934 96	1652 71	1467 88
145000	12571 46	6516 71	4502 09	3497 49	2896 90	2215 12	2004 06	1711 74	1520 30
150000	13004 96	6741 42	4657 33	3618 10	2996 80	2291 50	2073 17	1770 76	1572 72

94

MONTHLY PAYMENT

NECESSARY TO AMORTIZE A LOAN

7⅜%

AMOUNT	15 YEARS	18 YEARS	20 YEARS	25 YEARS	28 YEARS	29 YEARS	30 YEARS	35 YEARS	40 YEARS
50	46	42	40	37	36	35	35	34	33
100	92	84	80	74	71	70	70	67	65
200	1 84	1 68	1 60	1 47	1 41	1 40	1 39	1 34	1 30
300	2 76	2 52	2 40	2 20	2 12	2 10	2 08	2 00	1 95
400	3 68	3 36	3 20	2 93	2 82	2 79	2 77	2 67	2 60
500	4 60	4 19	3 99	3 66	3 53	3 49	3 46	3 33	3 25
600	5 52	5 03	4 79	4 39	4 23	4 19	4 15	4 00	3 90
700	6 44	5 87	5 59	5 12	4 94	4 89	4 84	4 66	4 55
800	7 36	6 71	6 39	5 85	5 64	5 58	5 53	5 33	5 20
900	8 28	7 54	7 19	6 58	6 35	6 28	6 22	5 99	5 84
1000	9 20	8 38	7 98	7 31	7 05	6 98	6 91	6 66	6 49
2000	18 40	16 76	15 96	14 62	14 09	13 95	13 82	13 31	12 98
3000	27 60	25 13	23 94	21 93	21 14	20 92	20 73	19 97	19 47
4000	36 80	33 51	31 92	29 24	28 18	27 90	27 63	26 62	25 96
5000	46 00	41 88	39 90	36 55	35 23	34 87	34 54	33 27	32 45
6000	55 20	50 26	47 88	43 86	42 27	41 84	41 45	39 93	38 94
7000	64 40	58 63	55 86	51 17	49 32	48 81	48 35	46 58	45 42
8000	73 60	67 01	63 84	58 48	56 36	55 79	55 26	53 23	51 91
9000	82 80	75 39	71 82	65 78	63 41	62 76	62 17	59 89	58 40
10000	92 00	83 76	79 80	73 09	70 45	69 73	69 07	66 54	64 89
15000	137 99	125 64	119 70	109 64	105 68	104 59	103 61	99 81	97 33
20000	183 99	167 52	159 60	146 18	140 90	139 46	138 14	133 07	129 78
25000	229 99	209 39	199 50	182 72	176 13	174 32	172 67	166 34	162 22
30000	275 98	251 27	239 40	219 27	211 35	209 18	207 21	199 61	194 66
35000	321 98	293 15	279 29	255 81	246 58	244 05	241 74	232 87	227 10
40000	367 97	335 03	319 19	292 35	281 80	278 91	276 28	266 14	259 55
45000	413 97	376 91	359 09	328 90	317 03	313 77	310 81	299 41	291 99
46000	423 17	385 28	367 07	336 21	324 07	320 75	317 72	306 06	298 48
47000	432 37	393 66	375 05	343 52	331 12	327 72	324 62	312 71	304 97
48000	441 57	402 03	383 03	350 83	338 16	334 69	331 53	319 37	311 45
49000	450 77	410 41	391 01	358 14	345 21	341 66	338 44	326 02	317 94
50000	459 97	418 78	398 99	365 44	352 25	348 64	345 34	332 67	324 43
51000	469 17	427 16	406 97	372 75	359 30	355 61	352 25	339 33	330 92
52000	478 37	435 53	414 95	380 06	366 34	362 58	359 16	345 98	337 41
53000	487 56	443 91	422 93	387 37	373 39	369 55	366 06	352 63	343 90
54000	496 76	452 29	430 91	394 68	380 43	376 53	372 97	359 29	350 39
55000	505 96	460 66	438 89	401 99	387 48	383 50	379 88	365 94	356 87
56000	515 16	469 04	446 87	409 30	394 52	390 47	386 78	372 59	363 36
57000	524 36	477 41	454 85	416 61	401 57	397 44	393 69	379 25	369 85
58000	533 56	485 79	462 83	423 92	408 61	404 42	400 60	385 90	376 34
59000	542 76	494 16	470 81	431 22	415 66	411 39	407 50	392 55	382 83
60000	551 96	502 54	478 79	438 53	422 70	418 36	414 41	399 21	389 32
61000	561 16	510 91	486 76	445 84	429 75	425 33	421 32	405 86	395 80
62000	570 36	519 29	494 74	453 15	436 79	432 31	428 22	412 51	402 29
63000	579 56	527 67	502 72	460 46	443 84	439 28	435 13	419 17	408 78
64000	588 76	536 04	510 70	467 77	450 88	446 25	442 04	425 82	415 27
65000	597 96	544 42	518 68	475 08	457 92	453 22	448 94	432 47	421 76
87500	620 85	565 36	538 63	493 35	475 54	470 66	466 21	449 11	437 98
70000	643 95	586 29	558 58	511 62	493 15	488 09	483 48	465 76	454 20
75000	689 95	628 17	598 48	548 16	528 37	522 95	518 01	499 01	486 64
80000	735 94	670 05	638 38	584 71	563 60	557 81	552 55	532 27	519 09
85000	781 94	711 93	678 28	621 25	598 82	592 68	587 08	565 54	551 53
90000	827 94	753 81	718 18	657 80	634 05	627 54	621 61	598 81	583 97
95000	873 93	795 68	758 07	694 34	669 27	662 40	656 15	632 07	616 41
100000	919 93	837 56	797 97	730 88	704 50	697 27	690 68	665 34	648 86
105000	965 92	879 44	837 87	767 43	739 72	732 13	725 21	698 61	681 30
110000	1011 92	921 32	877 77	803 97	774 95	766 99	759 75	731 87	713 74
115000	1057 92	963 19	917 67	840 52	810 17	801 86	794 28	765 14	746 18
120000	1103 91	1005 07	957 57	877 06	845 40	836 72	828 82	798 41	778 63
125000	1149 91	1046 95	997 46	913 60	880 62	871 58	863 35	831 67	811 07
130000	1195 91	1088 83	1037 36	950 15	915 84	906 44	897 88	864 94	843 51
135000	1241 90	1130 71	1077 26	986 69	951 07	941 31	932 42	898 21	875 96
140000	1287 90	1172 58	1117 16	1023 24	986 29	976 17	966 95	931 47	908 40
145000	1333 89	1214 46	1157 06	1059 78	1021 52	1011 03	1001 48	964 74	940 84
150000	1379 89	1256 34	1196 96	1096 32	1056 74	1045 90	1036 02	998 01	973 28

95

7½% MONTHLY PAYMENT
NECESSARY TO AMORTIZE A LOAN

AMOUNT	1 YEAR	2 YEARS	3 YEARS	4 YEARS	5 YEARS	7 YEARS	8 YEARS	10 YEARS	12 YEARS
50	4 34	2 25	1 56	1 21	1 01	77	70	60	53
100	8 68	4 50	3 12	2 42	2 01	1 54	1 39	1 19	1 06
200	17 36	9 00	6 23	4 84	4 01	3 07	2 78	2 38	2 12
300	26 03	13 50	9 34	7 26	6 02	4 61	4 17	3 57	3 17
400	34 71	18 00	12 45	9 68	8 02	6 14	5 56	4 75	4 23
500	43 38	22 50	15 56	12 09	10 02	7 67	6 95	5 94	5 28
600	52 06	27 00	18 67	14 51	12 03	9 21	8 34	7 13	6 34
700	60 74	31 50	21 78	16 93	14 03	10 74	9 72	8 31	7 39
800	69 41	36 08	24 89	19 35	16 04	12 28	11 11	9 50	8 45
900	78 09	40 50	28 00	21 77	18 04	13 81	12 50	10 69	9 50
1000	86 76	45 00	31 11	24 18	20 04	15 34	13 89	11 88	10 56
2000	173 52	90 00	62 22	48 36	40 08	30 68	27 77	23 75	21 11
3000	260 28	135 00	93 32	72 54	60 12	46 02	41 66	35 62	31 66
4000	347 03	180 00	124 43	96 72	80 16	61 36	55 54	47 49	42 21
5000	433 79	225 00	155 54	120 90	100 19	76 70	69 42	59 36	52 77
6000	520 55	270 00	186 64	145 08	120 23	92 03	83 31	71 23	63 32
7000	607 31	315 00	217 75	169 26	140 27	107 37	97 19	83 10	73 87
8000	694 06	360 00	248 85	193 44	160 31	122 71	111 08	94 97	84 42
9000	780 82	405 00	279 96	217 62	180 35	138 05	124 96	106 84	94 98
10000	867 58	450 00	311 07	241 79	200 38	153 39	138 84	118 71	105 53
15000	1301 37	675 00	466 60	362 69	300 57	230 08	208 26	178 06	158 29
20000	1735 15	900 00	622 13	483 58	400 76	306 77	277 68	237 41	211 06
25000	2168 94	1124 99	777 66	604 48	500 95	383 46	347 10	296 76	263 81
30000	2602 73	1349 99	933 19	725 37	601 14	460 15	416 52	356 11	316 57
35000	3036 51	1574 99	1088 72	846 27	701 33	536 84	485 94	415 46	369 33
40000	3470 30	1799 99	1244 25	967 16	801 52	613 54	555 36	474 81	422 10
45000	3904 09	2024 99	1399 78	1088 06	901 71	690 23	624 78	534 16	474 88
46000	3990 85	2069 99	1430 89	1112 23	921 75	705 57	638 66	546 03	485 41
47000	4077 60	2114 99	1462 00	1136 41	941 79	720 90	652 55	557 90	495 96
48000	4164 36	2159 99	1493 10	1160 59	961 83	736 24	666 43	569 77	506 51
49000	4251 12	2204 99	1524 21	1184 77	981 86	751 58	680 31	581 64	517 07
50000	4337 88	2249 99	1555 32	1208 95	1001 90	766 92	694 20	593 51	527 62
51000	4424 63	2294 98	1586 42	1233 13	1021 94	782 26	708 08	605 38	538 17
52000	4511 39	2339 98	1617 53	1257 31	1041 98	797 60	721 97	617 25	548 72
53000	4598 15	2384 98	1648 63	1281 49	1062 02	812 93	735 85	629 12	559 27
54000	4684 91	2429 98	1679 74	1305 67	1082 05	828 27	749 73	640 99	569 83
55000	4771 66	2474 98	1710 85	1329 84	1102 09	843 61	763 62	652 86	580 38
56000	4858 42	2519 98	1741 95	1354 02	1122 13	858 95	777 50	664 73	590 93
57000	4945 18	2564 98	1773 06	1378 20	1142 17	874 29	791 39	676 61	601 48
58000	5031 94	2609 98	1804 17	1402 38	1162 21	889 62	805 27	688 48	612 04
59000	5118 69	2654 98	1835 27	1426 56	1182 24	904 96	819 15	700 35	622 59
60000	5205 45	2699 98	1866 38	1450 74	1202 28	920 30	833 04	712 22	633 14
61000	5292 21	2744 98	1897 48	1474 92	1222 32	935 64	846 92	724 09	643 69
62000	5378 96	2789 98	1928 59	1499 10	1242 36	950 98	860 80	735 96	654 25
63000	5465 72	2834 98	1959 70	1523 28	1262 40	966 32	874 69	747 83	664 80
64000	5552 48	2879 98	1990 80	1547 45	1282 43	981 65	888 57	759 70	675 35
65000	5639 24	2924 98	2021 91	1571 63	1302 47	996 99	902 46	771 57	685 90
67500	5856 13	3037 48	2099 67	1632 08	1352 57	1035 34	937 17	801 24	712 28
70000	6073 02	3149 98	2177 44	1692 53	1402 66	1073 68	971 88	830 92	738 66
75000	6506 81	3374 97	2332 97	1813 42	1502 85	1150 38	1041 30	890 27	791 42
80000	6940 60	3599 97	2488 50	1934 32	1603 04	1227 07	1110 71	949 62	844 19
85000	7374 39	3824 97	2644 03	2055 21	1703 23	1303 76	1180 13	1008 97	896 95
90000	7808 17	4049 97	2799 56	2176 11	1803 42	1380 45	1249 55	1068 32	949 71
95000	8241 96	4274 97	2955 10	2297 00	1903 61	1457 14	1318 97	1127 67	1002 47
100000	8675 75	4499 96	3110 63	2417 90	2003 80	1533 83	1388 39	1187 02	1055 23
105000	9109 53	4724 96	3266 16	2538 79	2103 99	1610 52	1457 81	1246 37	1107 99
110000	9543 32	4949 96	3421 69	2659 68	2204 18	1687 22	1527 23	1305 72	1160 75
115000	9977 11	5174 96	3577 22	2780 58	2304 37	1763 91	1596 65	1365 08	1213 52
120000	10410 90	5399 96	3732 75	2901 47	2404 56	1840 60	1666 07	1424 43	1268 28
125000	10844 68	5624 95	3888 28	3022 37	2504 75	1917 29	1735 49	1483 78	1319 04
130000	11278 47	5849 95	4043 81	3143 26	2604 94	1993 98	1804 91	1543 13	1371 80
135000	11712 26	6074 95	4199 34	3264 16	2705 13	2070 67	1874 33	1602 48	1424 56
140000	12146 04	6299 95	4354 88	3385 05	2805 32	2147 36	1943 75	1661 83	1477 32
145000	12579 83	6524 95	4510 41	3505 95	2905 51	2224 05	2013 17	1721 18	1530 08
150000	13013 62	6749 94	4665 94	3626 84	3005 70	2300 75	2082 59	1780 53	1582 84

96

MONTHLY PAYMENT   7½%

NECESSARY TO AMORTIZE A LOAN

AMOUNT	15 YEARS	18 YEARS	20 YEARS	25 YEARS	28 YEARS	29 YEARS	30 YEARS	35 YEARS	40 YEARS
50	47	43	41	37	36	36	35	34	33
100	93	85	81	74	72	71	70	68	66
200	1 86	1 69	1 62	1 48	1 43	1 42	1 40	1 35	1 32
300	2 79	2 54	2 42	2 22	2 14	2 12	2 10	2 03	1 98
400	3 71	3 38	3 23	2 96	2 86	2 83	2 80	2 70	2 64
500	4 64	4 23	4 03	3 70	3 57	3 53	3 50	3 38	3 30
600	5 57	5 07	4 84	4 44	4 28	4 24	4 20	4 05	3 95
700	6 49	5 92	5 64	5 18	5 00	4 95	4 90	4 72	4 61
800	7 42	6 76	6 45	5 92	5 71	5 65	5 60	5 40	5 27
900	8 35	7 61	7 26	6 66	6 42	6 36	6 30	6 07	5 93
1000	9 28	8 45	8 06	7 39	7 13	7 06	7 00	6 75	6 59
2000	18 55	16 90	16 12	14 78	14 26	14 12	13 99	13 49	13 17
3000	27 82	25 35	24 17	22 17	21 39	21 18	20 98	20 23	19 75
4000	37 09	33 80	32 23	29 56	28 52	28 23	27 97	26 97	26 33
5000	46 36	42 25	40 28	36 95	35 65	35 29	34 97	33 72	32 91
6000	55 63	50 70	48 34	44 34	42 78	42 35	41 96	40 46	39 49
7000	64 90	59 15	56 40	51 73	49 91	49 41	48 96	47 20	46 07
8000	74 17	67 60	64 45	59 12	57 03	56 46	55 94	53 94	52 65
9000	83 44	76 05	72 51	66 51	64 16	63 52	62 93	60 69	59 23
10000	92 71	84 50	80 56	73 90	71 29	70 58	69 93	67 43	65 81
15000	139 06	126 75	120 84	110 85	106 94	105 86	104 89	101 14	98 72
20000	185 41	169 00	161 12	147 80	142 58	141 15	139 85	134 85	131 62
25000	231 76	211 25	201 40	184 75	178 22	176 44	174 81	168 57	164 52
30000	278 11	253 50	241 68	221 70	213 87	211 72	209 77	202 28	197 43
35000	324 46	295 75	281 96	258 65	249 51	247 01	244 73	235 99	230 33
40000	370 81	337 99	322 24	295	285 15	282 29	279 69	269 70	263 23
45000	417 16	380 24	362 52	332 55	320 80	317 58	314 65	303 41	296 14
46000	426 43	388 69	370 58	339 94	327 92	324 64	321 64	310 16	302 72
47000	435 70	397 11	378 63	347 33	335 05	331 69	328 64	316 90	309 30
48000	444 97	405 59	386 69	354 72	342 18	338 75	335 53	323 64	315 88
49000	454 24	414 04	394 75	362 11	349 31	345 81	342 62	330 38	322 46
50000	463 51	422 49	402 80	369 50	356 44	352 87	349 62	337 13	329 04
51000	472 78	430 94	410 86	376 89	363 57	359 92	356 60	343 87	335 62
52000	482 05	439 39	418 91	384 28	370 70	366 98	363 60	350 61	342 20
53000	491 32	447 84	426 97	391 67	377 82	374 04	370 59	357 35	348 78
54000	500 59	456 29	435 03	399 06	384 95	381 09	377 58	364 10	355 36
55000	509 86	464 74	443 08	406 45	392 08	388 15	384 57	370 84	361 94
56000	519 13	473 19	451 14	413 84	399 21	395 21	391 57	377 58	368 52
57000	528 40	481 64	459 19	421 23	406 34	402 27	398 56	384 32	375 11
58000	537 67	490 09	467 25	428 62	413 47	409 32	405 55	391 07	381 69
59000	546 94	498 54	475 30	436 01	420 60	416 38	412 54	397 81	388 27
60000	556 21	506 99	483 36	443 40	427 73	423 44	419 53	404 55	394 85
61000	565 48	515 44	491 42	450 79	434 85	430 49	426 53	411 29	401 43
62000	574 75	523 89	499 47	458 18	441 98	437 55	433 52	418 04	408 01
63000	584 02	532 34	507 53	465 57	449 11	444 61	440 51	424 78	414 59
64000	593 29	540 79	515 58	472 98	456 24	451 67	447 50	431 52	421 17
65000	602 56	549 24	523 64	480 35	463 37	458 72	454 49	438 26	427 75
67500	625 74	570 36	543 78	498 82	481 19	476 37	471 97	455 12	444 20
70000	648 91	591 49	563 92	517 30	499 01	494 01	489 45	471 97	460 65
75000	695 26	633 73	604 20	554 25	534 65	529 30	524 42	505 69	493 56
80000	741 61	675 98	644 48	591 20	570 30	564 58	559 38	539 40	526 46
85000	787 97	718 23	684 76	628 15	605 94	599 87	594 34	573 11	559 37
90000	834 32	760 48	725 04	665 10	641 59	635 15	629 30	606 82	592 27
95000	880 67	802 73	765 32	702 05	677 23	670 44	664 26	640 54	625 17
100000	927 02	844 98	805 60	739 00	712 87	705 73	699 22	674 25	658 08
105000	973 37	887 23	845 88	775 95	748 52	741 01	734 18	707 96	690 98
110000	1019 72	929 48	886 16	812 90	784 16	776 30	769 14	741 67	723 88
115000	1066 07	971 72	926 44	849 84	819 80	811 58	804 10	775 38	756 79
120000	1112 42	1013 97	966 72	886 79	855 45	846 87	839 06	809 10	789 69
125000	1158 77	1056 22	1007 00	923 74	891 09	882 16	874 02	842 81	822 59
130000	1205 12	1098 47	1047 28	960 69	926 73	917 44	908 98	876 52	855 50
135000	1251 47	1140 72	1087 56	997 64	962 38	952 73	943 94	910 23	888 40
140000	1297 82	1182 97	1127 84	1034 59	998 02	988 01	978 91	943 94	921 30
145000	1344 17	1225 22	1168 12	1071 54	1033 66	1023 30	1013 87	977 66	954 21
150000	1390 52	1267 46	1208 39	1108 49	1069 31	1058 59	1048 83	1011 37	987 11

97

MONTHLY PAYMENT
NECESSARY TO AMORTIZE A LOAN

AMOUNT	1 YEAR	2 YEARS	3 YEARS	4 YEARS	5 YEARS	7 YEARS	8 YEARS	10 YEARS	12 YEARS
50	4 35	2 26	1 56	1 22	1 01	.78	.70	60	54
100	8 69	4 51	3 12	2 43	2 01	1 55	1 40	1 20	1 07
200	17 37	9 02	6 24	4 85	4 02	3 09	2 79	2 39	2 13
300	26 05	13 52	9 35	7 28	6 03	4 63	4 19	3 59	3 19
400	34 73	18 03	12 47	9 70	8 04	6 17	5 58	4 78	4 25
500	43 41	22 53	15 59	12 12	10 05	7 71	6 98	5 97	5 31
600	52 09	27 04	18 70	14 55	12 06	9 25	8 37	7 17	6 38
700	60 78	31 54	21 82	16 97	14 07	10 79	9 77	8 36	7 44
800	69 46	36 05	24 94	19 39	16 08	12 33	11 18	9 55	8 50
900	78 14	40 56	28 05	21 82	18 09	13 87	12 56	10 75	9 56
1000	86 82	45 06	31 17	24 24	20 10	15 41	13 95	11 94	10 62
2000	173 64	90 12	62 33	48 48	40 20	30 81	27 90	23 88	21 24
3000	260 45	135 17	93 50	72 72	60 30	46 21	41 85	35 81	31 86
4000	347 27	180 23	124 66	96 95	80 39	61 61	55 79	47 75	42 48
5000	434 08	225 29	155 82	121 19	100 49	77 01	69 74	59 68	53 10
6000	520 90	270 34	186 99	145 43	120 59	92 41	83 69	71 62	63 72
7000	607 71	315 40	218 15	169 67	140 69	107 81	97 63	83 55	74 34
8000	694 53	360 46	249 31	193 90	160 78	123 21	111 58	95 49	84 96
9000	781 34	405 51	280 48	218 14	180 88	138 61	125 52	107 42	95 58
10000	868 16	450 57	311 64	242 38	200 98	154 01	139 47	119 36	106 20
15000	1302 23	675 85	467 46	363 56	301 47	231 01	209 21	179 04	159 30
20000	1736 31	901 13	623 28	484 75	401 96	308 01	278 94	238 72	212 40
25000	2170 38	1126 42	779 10	605 94	502 44	385 01	348 68	298 39	265 50
30000	2604 46	1351 70	934 91	727 12	602 93	462 01	418 41	358 07	318 60
35000	3038 53	1576 99	1090 73	848 31	703 41	539 01	488 14	417 75	371 70
40000	3472 61	1802 26	1246 55	969 50	803 90	616 01	557 88	477 43	424 80
45000	3906 69	2027 55	1402 37	1090 68	904 39	693 01	627 61	537 10	477 90
46000	3993 50	2072 60	1433 53	1114 92	924 49	708 41	641 56	549 04	488 52
47000	4080 32	2117 66	1464 70	1139 16	944 58	723 81	655 51	560 97	499 14
48000	4167 13	2162 71	1495 86	1163 39	964 68	739 21	669 45	572 91	509 76
49000	4253 95	2207 77	1527 02	1187 63	984 78	754 61	683 40	584 85	520 38
50000	4340 76	2252 83	1558 19	1211 87	1004 88	770 01	697 35	596 78	531 00
51000	4427 58	2297 88	1589 35	1236 11	1024 97	785 41	711 29	608 72	541 62
52000	4514 39	2342 94	1620 52	1260 34	1045 07	800 81	725 24	620 65	552 24
53000	4601 21	2388 00	1651 68	1284 58	1065 17	816 21	739 19	632 59	562 86
54000	4688 02	2433 05	1682 84	1308 82	1085 26	831 61	753 13	644 52	573 48
55000	4774 84	2478 11	1714 01	1333 06	1105 36	847 01	767 08	656 46	584 10
56000	4861 65	2523 17	1745 17	1357 29	1125 46	862 41	781 03	668 39	594 72
57000	4948 47	2568 22	1776 33	1381 53	1145 56	877 81	794 97	680 33	605 34
58000	5035 28	2613 28	1807 50	1405 77	1165 65	893 21	808 92	692 27	615 96
59000	5122 10	2658 34	1838 66	1430 00	1185 75	908 61	822 87	704 20	626 58
60000	5208 91	2703 39	1869 82	1454 24	1205 85	924 01	836 81	716 14	637 20
61000	5295 73	2748 45	1900 99	1478 48	1225 95	939 41	850 76	728 07	647 82
62000	5382 54	2793 51	1932 15	1502 72	1246 04	954 81	864 71	740 01	658 44
63000	5469 36	2838 56	1963 32	1526 95	1266 14	970 21	878 65	751 94	669 06
64000	5556 17	2883 62	1994 48	1551 19	1286 24	985 61	892 60	763 88	679 68
65000	5642 99	2928 67	2025 64	1575 43	1306 34	1001 01	906 55	775 81	690 30
67500	5860 03	3041 32	2103 55	1636 02	1356 58	1039 51	941 42	805 65	716 85
70000	6077 06	3153 96	2181 46	1696 61	1406 82	1078 01	976 28	835 49	743 40
75000	6511 14	3379 24	2337 28	1817 80	1507 31	1155 01	1046 02	895 17	796 50
80000	6945 22	3604 52	2493 10	1938 99	1607 80	1232 01	1115 75	954 85	849 60
85000	7379 29	3829 80	2648 92	2060 17	1708 28	1309 01	1185 49	1014 52	902 70
90000	7813 37	4055 09	2804 73	2181 36	1808 77	1386 01	1255 22	1074 20	955 80
95000	8247 44	4280 37	2960 55	2302 55	1909 26	1463 01	1324 95	1133 88	1008 90
100000	8681 52	4505 65	3116 37	2423 73	2009 75	1540 01	1394 69	1193 56	1062 00
105000	9115 59	4730 93	3272 19	2544 92	2110 23	1617 01	1464 42	1253 23	1115 10
110000	9549 67	4956 21	3428 01	2666 11	2210 72	1694 01	1534 16	1312 91	1168 20
115000	9983 75	5181 50	3583 83	2787 29	2311 21	1771 01	1603 89	1372 59	1221 30
120000	10417 82	5406 78	3739 64	2908 48	2411 69	1848 01	1673 62	1432 27	1274 40
125000	10851 90	5632 06	3895 46	3029 66	2512 18	1925 01	1743 36	1491 94	1327 50
130000	11285 97	5857 34	4051 28	3150 85	2612 67	2002 01	1813 09	1551 62	1380 60
135000	11720 05	6082 63	4207 10	3272 04	2713 15	2079 01	1882 83	1611 30	1433 70
140000	12154 12	6307 91	4362 92	3393 22	2813 64	2156 01	1952 56	1670 98	1486 80
145000	12588 20	6533 19	4518 74	3514 41	2914 13	2233 01	2022 29	1730 66	1539 90
150000	13022 28	6758 47	4674 55	3635 60	3014 62	2310 01	2092 03	1790 33	1593 00

AMOUNT	15 YEARS	18 YEARS	20 YEARS	25 YEARS	28 YEARS	29 YEARS	30 YEARS	35 YEARS	40 YEARS
50	47	43	41	38	37	36	36	35	34
100	94	86	82	75	73	72	71	69	67
200	187	171	163	150	145	143	142	137	134
300	281	256	244	225	217	215	213	205	201
400	374	341	326	299	289	286	284	274	267
500	468	427	407	374	361	358	354	342	334
600	561	512	488	449	433	429	425	410	401
700	654	597	570	523	505	500	496	479	468
800	748	682	651	598	578	572	567	547	534
900	841	768	732	673	650	643	638	615	601
1000	935	853	814	748	722	715	708	684	668
2000	1869	1705	1627	1495	1443	1429	1416	1367	1335
3000	2803	2558	2440	2242	2164	2143	2124	2050	2002
4000	3737	3410	3254	2989	2886	2857	2832	2733	2670
5000	4671	4263	4067	3736	3607	3572	3539	3416	3337
6000	5605	5115	4880	4483	4328	4286	4247	4100	4004
7000	6539	5967	5693	5230	5049	5000	4955	4783	4672
8000	7474	6820	6507	5978	5771	5714	5663	5466	5339
9000	8408	7672	7320	6725	6492	6428	6371	6149	6006
10000	9342	8525	8133	7472	7213	7143	7078	6832	6674
15000	14012	12787	12199	11208	10820	10714	10617	10248	10010
20000	18683	17049	16266	14943	14426	14285	14156	13664	13347
25000	23354	21311	20332	18679	18033	17856	17695	17080	16684
30000	28024	25573	24398	22415	21639	21427	21234	20496	20020
35000	32695	29835	28464	26150	25245	24998	24773	23912	23357
40000	37366	34097	32531	29886	28852	28569	28312	27328	26694
45000	42036	38360	36597	33622	32458	32140	31851	30744	30030
46000	42970	39212	37410	34369	33179	32855	32559	31427	30698
47000	43905	40064	38223	35116	33901	33569	33267	32110	31365
48000	44839	40917	39037	35862	34622	34283	33975	32794	32032
49000	45773	41769	39850	36610	35343	34997	34682	33477	32700
50000	46707	42622	40663	37358	36065	35711	35390	34160	33367
51000	47641	43474	41478	38105	36786	36425	36098	34843	34034
52000	48575	44326	42290	38852	37507	37140	36806	35526	34702
53000	49509	45179	43103	39599	38228	37854	37514	36210	35369
54000	50444	46031	43916	40346	38950	38568	38221	36893	36036
55000	51378	46884	44729	41093	39671	39283	38929	37576	36703
56000	52312	47736	45543	41840	40392	39997	39637	38259	37371
57000	53246	48589	46356	42588	41114	40711	40345	38942	38038
58000	54180	49441	47169	43335	41835	41425	41052	39626	38705
59000	55114	50293	47982	44082	42556	42139	41760	40309	39373
60000	56048	51146	48796	44829	43277	42854	42468	40992	40040
61000	56982	51998	49609	45576	43999	43568	43176	41675	40707
62000	57917	52851	50422	46323	44720	44282	43884	42358	41375
63000	58851	53703	51235	47070	45441	44996	44592	43041	42042
64000	59785	54556	52049	47818	46163	45710	45299	43725	42709
65000	60719	55408	52862	48565	46884	46425	46007	44408	43377
67500	63054	57539	54895	50433	48687	48210	47777	46118	45045
70000	65390	59670	56928	52300	50490	49996	49546	47824	46713
75000	70060	63932	60995	56038	54097	53567	53085	51240	50050
80000	74731	68194	65061	59772	57703	57138	56624	54656	53387
85000	79402	72456	69127	63507	61310	60709	60163	58072	56723
90000	84072	76719	73193	67243	64918	64280	63702	61488	60060
95000	88743	80981	77260	70979	68522	67851	67241	64904	63397
100000	93413	85243	81326	74715	72129	71422	70780	68319	66733
105000	98084	89505	85392	78450	75735	74993	74319	71735	70070
110000	102755	93767	89458	82186	79342	78565	77858	75151	73406
115000	107425	98029	93525	85922	92948	82136	81397	78567	76743
120000	112096	102291	97591	89657	86554	85707	84936	81983	80080
125000	116767	106553	101657	93393	90161	89278	88475	85399	83416
130000	121437	110815	105723	97129	93767	92849	92014	88815	86753
135000	126108	115078	109790	100865	97374	96420	95553	92231	90090
140000	130779	119340	113856	104600	100980	99991	99092	95647	93426
145000	135449	123602	117922	108336	104586	103562	102631	99063	96763
150000	140120	127864	121989	112072	108193	107133	106170	102479	100100

7¾% MONTHLY PAYMENT

NECESSARY TO AMORTIZE A LOAN

AMOUNT	1 YEAR	2 YEARS	3 YEARS	4 YEARS	5 YEARS	7 YEARS	8 YEARS	10 YEARS	12 YEARS
50	4.35	2.28	1.57	1.22	1.01	.78	.71	.61	.54
100	8.68	4.52	3.13	2.43	2.02	1.55	1.41	1.21	1.07
200	17.38	9.03	6.25	4.86	4.04	3.10	2.81	2.41	2.14
300	26.07	13.54	9.37	7.29	6.05	4.64	4.21	3.61	3.21
400	34.75	18.05	12.49	9.72	8.07	6.19	5.61	4.81	4.28
500	43.44	22.56	15.62	12.15	10.08	7.74	7.01	6.01	5.35
600	52.13	27.07	18.74	14.58	12.10	9.28	8.41	7.21	6.42
700	60.82	31.58	21.86	17.01	14.11	10.83	9.81	8.41	7.49
800	69.50	36.10	24.98	19.44	16.13	12.37	11.21	9.61	8.56
900	78.19	40.61	28.10	21.87	18.15	13.92	12.61	10.81	9.62
1000	86.88	45.12	31.23	24.30	20.16	15.47	14.01	12.01	10.69
2000	173.75	90.23	62.45	48.60	40.32	30.93	28.02	24.01	21.38
3000	260.62	135.35	93.67	72.89	60.48	46.39	42.03	36.01	32.07
4000	347.50	180.46	124.89	97.19	80.63	61.85	56.04	48.01	42.76
5000	434.37	225.57	156.11	121.48	100.79	77.31	70.05	60.01	53.44
6000	521.24	270.69	187.33	145.78	120.95	92.78	84.06	72.01	64.13
7000	608.12	315.80	218.55	170.08	141.10	108.24	98.07	84.01	74.82
8000	694.99	360.91	249.77	194.37	161.26	123.70	112.08	96.01	85.51
9000	781.86	406.03	281.00	218.67	181.42	139.16	126.09	108.01	96.20
10000	868.73	451.14	312.22	242.96	201.57	154.62	140.10	120.02	106.88
15000	1303.10	676.71	468.32	364.44	302.36	231.93	210.15	180.02	160.32
20000	1737.46	902.27	624.43	485.92	403.14	309.24	280.20	240.03	213.76
25000	2171.83	1127.84	780.53	607.40	503.93	386.55	350.25	300.03	267.20
30000	2606.19	1353.41	936.64	728.88	604.71	463.86	420.30	360.04	320.64
35000	3040.56	1578.97	1092.75	850.36	705.50	541.17	490.35	420.04	374.08
40000	3474.92	1804.54	1248.85	971.83	806.28	618.48	560.40	480.05	427.52
45000	3909.28	2030.11	1404.96	1093.31	907.07	695.79	630.45	540.05	480.96
46000	3996.16	2075.22	1436.18	1117.61	927.23	711.25	644.46	552.05	491.65
47000	4083.03	2120.33	1467.40	1141.90	947.38	726.72	658.47	564.05	502.34
48000	4169.90	2165.45	1498.62	1166.20	967.54	742.18	672.48	576.06	513.03
49000	4256.78	2210.56	1529.84	1190.50	987.70	757.64	686.49	588.06	523.71
50000	4343.65	2255.67	1561.06	1214.79	1007.85	773.10	700.50	600.06	534.40
51000	4430.52	2300.79	1592.28	1239.09	1028.01	788.56	714.51	612.06	545.09
52000	4517.39	2345.90	1623.51	1263.38	1048.17	804.03	728.52	624.06	555.78
53000	4604.27	2391.01	1654.73	1287.68	1068.32	819.49	742.53	636.06	566.46
54000	4691.14	2436.13	1685.95	1311.98	1088.48	834.95	756.54	648.06	577.15
55000	4778.01	2481.24	1717.17	1336.27	1108.64	850.41	770.55	660.06	587.84
56000	4864.88	2526.35	1748.39	1360.57	1128.79	865.87	784.56	672.06	598.53
57000	4951.76	2571.47	1779.61	1384.86	1148.95	881.34	798.57	684.07	609.22
58000	5038.63	2616.58	1810.83	1409.16	1169.11	896.80	812.58	696.07	619.90
59000	5125.50	2661.69	1842.05	1433.45	1189.27	912.26	826.58	708.07	630.59
60000	5212.38	2706.81	1873.27	1457.75	1209.42	927.72	840.60	720.07	641.28
61000	5299.25	2751.92	1904.50	1482.05	1229.58	943.18	854.61	732.07	651.97
62000	5386.12	2797.03	1935.72	1506.34	1249.74	958.65	868.62	744.07	662.66
63000	5473.00	2842.15	1966.94	1530.64	1269.89	974.11	882.63	756.07	673.34
64000	5559.87	2887.26	1998.16	1554.93	1290.05	989.57	896.64	768.07	684.03
65000	5646.74	2932.37	2029.38	1579.23	1310.21	1005.03	910.65	780.07	694.72
67500	5863.92	3045.16	2107.43	1639.97	1360.60	1043.69	945.68	810.08	721.44
70000	6081.11	3157.94	2185.48	1700.71	1410.99	1082.34	980.70	840.08	748.16
75000	6515.47	3383.51	2341.59	1822.19	1511.78	1159.65	1050.75	900.08	801.60
80000	6949.84	3609.07	2497.70	1943.66	1612.58	1236.96	1120.80	960.09	855.04
85000	7384.20	3834.64	2653.80	2065.14	1713.35	1314.27	1190.85	1020.10	908.48
90000	7818.56	4060.21	2809.91	2186.62	1814.13	1391.58	1260.90	1080.10	961.92
95000	8252.93	4285.77	2966.02	2308.10	1914.92	1468.88	1330.95	1140.11	1015.36
100000	8687.29	4511.34	3122.12	2429.58	2015.70	1546.20	1401.00	1200.11	1068.80
105000	9121.66	4736.91	3278.23	2551.06	2116.49	1623.51	1471.05	1260.12	1122.24
110000	9556.02	4962.47	3434.33	2672.54	2217.27	1700.82	1541.10	1320.12	1175.68
115000	9990.39	5188.04	3590.44	2794.02	2318.06	1778.13	1611.15	1380.13	1229.12
120000	10424.75	5413.61	3746.54	2915.49	2418.84	1855.44	1681.20	1440.13	1282.56
125000	10859.12	5639.17	3902.65	3036.97	2519.62	1932.75	1751.25	1500.14	1336.00
130000	11293.48	5864.74	4058.76	3158.45	2620.41	2010.06	1821.30	1560.14	1389.44
135000	11727.84	6090.31	4214.86	3279.93	2721.19	2087.37	1891.35	1620.15	1442.87
140000	12162.21	6315.87	4370.97	3401.41	2821.98	2164.68	1961.40	1680.15	1496.31
145000	12596.57	6541.44	4527.07	3522.89	2922.76	2241.99	2031.45	1740.16	1549.75
150000	13030.94	6767.01	4683.18	3644.37	3023.55	2319.30	2101.50	1800.16	1603.19

7⅞% MONTHLY PAYMENT
NECESSARY TO AMORTIZE A LOAN

AMOUNT	1 YEAR	2 YEARS	3 YEARS	4 YEARS	5 YEARS	7 YEARS	8 YEARS	10 YEARS	12 YEARS
50	4 35	2 26	1 57	1 22	1 02	78	71	61	54
100	8 70	4 52	3 13	2 44	2 03	1 56	1 41	1 21	1 08
200	17 39	9 04	6 26	4 88	4 05	3 11	2 82	2 42	2 16
300	26 08	13 56	9 38	7 31	6 07	4 66	4 23	3 63	3 23
400	34 78	18 07	12 52	9 75	8 09	6 21	5 63	4 83	4 31
500	43 47	22 59	15 64	12 18	10 11	7 77	7 04	6 04	5 38
600	52 16	27 11	18 77	14 62	12 13	9 32	8 45	7 25	6 46
700	60 86	31 62	21 90	17 05	14 16	10 87	9 86	8 45	7 53
800	69 55	36 14	25 03	19 49	16 18	12 42	11 26	9 66	8 61
900	78 24	40 66	28 16	21 92	18 20	13 98	12 67	10 87	9 69
1000	86 94	45 18	31 28	24 36	20 22	15 53	14 08	12 07	10 76
2000	173 87	90 35	62 56	48 71	40 44	31 05	28 15	24 14	21 52
3000	260 80	135 52	93 84	73 07	60 65	46 58	42 22	36 21	32 27
4000	347 73	180 69	125 12	97 42	80 87	62 10	56 30	48 27	43 03
5000	434 66	225 86	156 40	121 78	101 09	77 63	70 37	60 34	53 78
6000	521 59	271 03	187 68	146 13	121 30	93 15	84 44	72 41	64 54
7000	608 52	316 20	218 96	170 49	141 52	108 67	98 52	84 47	75 30
8000	695 45	361 37	250 23	194 84	161 74	124 20	112 59	96 54	86 05
9000	782 38	406 54	281 51	219 19	181 95	139 72	126 66	108 61	96 81
10000	869 31	451 71	312 79	243 55	202 17	155 25	140 74	120 67	107 57
15000	1303 96	677 56	469 19	365 32	303 25	232 87	211 10	181 01	161 35
20000	1738 62	903 41	625 58	487 09	404 34	310 49	281 47	241 34	215 13
25000	2173 27	1129 26	781 97	608 86	505 42	388 11	351 84	301 68	268 91
30000	2607 92	1355 11	938 37	730 63	606 50	465 73	422 20	362 01	322 69
35000	3042 58	1580 97	1094 76	852 41	707 59	543 35	492 57	422 34	376 47
40000	3477 23	1806 82	1251 15	974 18	808 67	620 97	562 93	482 68	430 25
45000	3911 88	2032 67	1407 55	1095 95	909 75	698 59	633 30	543 01	484 03
46000	3998 81	2077 84	1438 83	1120 30	929 97	714 11	647 37	555 08	494 79
47000	4085 75	2123 01	1470 11	1144 66	950 19	729 63	661 45	567 15	505 54
48000	4172 68	2168 18	1501 38	1169 01	970 40	745 16	675 52	579 21	516 30
49000	4259 61	2213 35	1532 66	1193 37	990 62	760 68	689 59	591 28	527 06
50000	4346 54	2258 52	1563 94	1217 72	1010 84	776 21	703 67	603 35	537 81
51000	4433 47	2303 69	1595 22	1242 07	1031 06	791 73	717 74	615 41	548 57
52000	4520 40	2348 86	1626 50	1266 43	1051 27	807 25	731 81	627 48	559 32
53000	4607 33	2394 03	1657 78	1290 78	1071 49	822 78	745 89	639 55	570 08
54000	4694 26	2439 20	1689 06	1315 14	1091 70	838 30	759 96	651 61	580 83
55000	4781 19	2484 37	1720 34	1339 49	1111 92	853 83	774 03	663 68	591 59
56000	4868 12	2529 54	1751 61	1363 85	1132 14	869 35	788 11	675 75	602 35
57000	4955 06	2574 71	1782 89	1388 20	1152 35	884 87	802 18	687 81	613 10
58000	5041 98	2619 88	1814 17	1412 55	1172 57	900 40	816 25	699 88	623 86
59000	5128 91	2665 05	1845 45	1436 91	1192 79	915 92	830 33	711 95	634 62
60000	5215 84	2710 22	1876 73	1461 26	1213 00	931 45	844 40	724 01	645 37
61000	5302 77	2755 39	1908 01	1485 62	1233 22	946 97	858 47	736 08	656 13
62000	5389 70	2800 56	1939 29	1509 97	1253 44	962 49	872 55	748 15	666 88
63000	5476 64	2845 73	1970 57	1534 33	1273 65	978 02	886 62	760 21	677 64
64000	5563 57	2890 90	2001 84	1558 68	1293 87	993 54	900 69	772 28	688 40
65000	5650 50	2938 07	2033 12	1583 03	1314 09	1009 07	914 76	784 35	699 15
87500	5887 82	3049 00	2111 32	1643 92	1364 63	1047 88	949 95	814 51	726 04
70000	6085 15	3161 93	2189 52	1704 81	1415 17	1086 69	985 13	844 68	752 93
75000	6519 80	3387 78	2345 91	1826 58	1516 25	1164 31	1055 50	905 02	806 71
80000	6954 46	3613 63	2502 30	1948 35	1617 33	1241 93	1125 86	965 35	860 49
85000	7389 11	3839 48	2658 70	2070 12	1718 42	1319 55	1196 23	1025 68	914 27
90000	7823 76	4065 33	2815 09	2191 89	1819 50	1397 17	1266 60	1086 02	968 05
95000	8258 42	4291 18	2971 48	2313 66	1920 58	1474 79	1336 96	1146 35	1021 83
100000	8693 07	4517 04	3127 88	2435 43	2021 67	1552 41	1407 33	1206 69	1075 62
105000	9127 72	4742 89	3284 27	2557 21	2122 75	1630 03	1477 69	1267 02	1129 40
110000	9562 38	4968 74	3440 67	2678 98	2223 83	1707 65	1548 06	1327 35	1183 18
115000	9997 03	5194 59	3597 06	2800 75	2324 92	1785 27	1618 43	1387 69	1236 96
120000	10431 68	5420 44	3753 45	2922 52	2426 00	1862 89	1688 79	1448 02	1290 74
125000	10866 34	5646 29	3909 85	3044 29	2527 08	1940 51	1759 16	1508 36	1344 52
130000	11300 99	5872 14	4066 24	3166 06	2628 17	2018 13	1829 52	1568 69	1398 30
135000	11735 64	6098 00	4222 63	3287 83	2729 25	2095 75	1899 89	1629 02	1452 08
140000	12170 30	6323 85	4379 03	3409 61	2830 33	2173 37	1970 26	1689 36	1505 86
145000	12604 95	6549 70	4535 42	3531 38	2931 42	2250 99	2040 62	1749 69	1559 64
150000	13039 60	6775 55	4691 81	3653 15	3032 50	2328 61	2110 99	1810 03	1613 42

101

MONTHLY PAYMENT 7⅞%
NECESSARY TO AMORTIZE A LOAN

AMOUNT	15 YEARS	18 YEARS	20 YEARS	25 YEARS	28 YEARS	29 YEARS	30 YEARS	35 YEARS	40 YEARS
50	48	44	42	39	37	37	37	36	35
100	95	87	83	77	74	74	73	71	69
200	190	174	166	153	148	147	146	161	138
300	285	261	249	230	222	220	219	211	206
400	380	347	332	306	296	293	291	281	275
500	475	434	415	382	370	366	363	351	343
600	570	521	498	459	443	439	436	421	412
700	664	608	581	535	517	512	508	491	481
800	759	694	663	611	591	586	581	561	549
900	854	781	746	688	665	659	653	632	618
1000	949	868	829	764	739	732	726	702	686
2000	1897	1735	1658	1528	1477	1463	1451	1403	1372
3000	2846	2603	2487	2291	2215	2194	2176	2104	2058
4000	3794	3470	3315	3055	2953	2926	2904	2805	2744
5000	4743	4338	4144	3818	3692	3657	3628	3506	3430
6000	5691	5205	4973	4582	4430	4388	4351	4208	4118
7000	6640	6072	5801	5345	5188	5120	5078	4909	4802
8000	7588	6940	6630	6109	5906	5851	5801	5610	5488
9000	8537	7807	7459	6872	6645	6582	6526	6311	6174
10000	9485	8675	8287	7636	7383	7314	7251	7012	6860
15000	14227	13012	12431	11454	11074	10970	10877	10518	10290
20000	18969	17349	16574	15272	14765	14627	14502	14024	13719
25000	23712	21686	20717	19089	18456	18284	18127	17530	17149
30000	28454	26023	24861	22907	22147	21940	21753	21036	20579
35000	33196	30360	29004	26725	25838	25597	25378	24542	24009
40000	37938	34697	33148	30543	29530	29254	29003	28048	27438
45000	42681	39034	37291	34360	33221	32910	32629	31554	30868
46000	43629	39902	38120	35124	33959	33642	33354	32256	31554
47000	44578	40769	38948	35888	34697	34373	34079	32957	32240
48000	45526	41637	39777	36651	35435	35104	34804	33658	32926
49000	46475	42504	40606	37415	36174	35836	35529	34359	33612
50000	47423	43371	41434	38178	36912	36567	36254	35060	34298
51000	48371	44239	42263	38942	37650	37288	36979	35762	34984
52000	49320	45106	43092	39705	38388	38030	37704	36463	35670
53000	50268	45974	43920	40469	39127	38761	38429	37164	36356
54000	51217	46841	44749	41232	39865	39492	39154	37865	37042
55000	52165	47708	45578	41996	40603	40224	39879	38566	37728
56000	53114	48576	46406	42760	41341	40955	40604	39268	38414
57000	54062	49443	47235	43523	42080	41686	41329	39968	39100
58000	55011	50311	48064	44287	42818	42418	42055	40670	39786
59000	55959	51178	48892	45050	43556	43149	42780	41371	40471
60000	56907	52046	49721	45814	44294	43880	43505	42072	41157
61000	57856	52913	50550	46577	45032	44612	44230	42774	41843
62000	58804	53780	51379	47341	45771	45343	44955	43475	42529
63000	59753	54648	52207	48104	46509	46074	45680	44176	43215
64000	60701	55515	53036	48868	47247	46806	46405	44877	43901
65000	61650	56383	53865	49632	47985	47537	47130	45578	44587
67500	64021	58551	55936	51540	49831	49365	48943	47331	46302
70000	66392	60720	58008	53449	51678	51194	50755	49084	48017
75000	71134	65057	62151	57267	55368	54850	54381	52590	51447
80000	75876	69394	66295	61085	59058	58507	58006	56096	54876
85000	80619	73731	70438	64903	62750	62164	61631	59602	58306
90000	85361	78068	74581	68721	66441	65820	65257	63108	61736
95000	90103	82405	78725	72538	70132	69477	68882	66614	65166
100000	94845	86742	82868	76356	73823	73134	72507	70120	68595
105000	99588	91079	87012	80174	77514	76790	76133	73626	72025
110000	104330	95416	91155	83991	81206	80447	79758	77132	75455
115000	109072	99754	95298	87809	84897	84104	83383	80638	78885
120000	113814	104091	99442	91627	88588	87760	87009	84144	82314
125000	118557	108428	103585	95445	92279	91417	90634	87650	85744
130000	123299	112765	107729	99263	95970	95074	94260	91156	89174
135000	128041	117102	111872	103080	99661	98730	97885	94662	92604
140000	132783	121439	116015	106898	103352	102387	101516	98168	96033
145000	137526	125776	120158	110716	107044	106044	105136	101674	99463
150000	142268	130113	124302	114534	110735	109700	108761	105180	102893

8% MONTHLY PAYMENT
NECESSARY TO AMORTIZE A LOAN

AMOUNT	1 YEAR	2 YEARS	3 YEARS	4 YEARS	5 YEARS	7 YEARS	8 YEARS	10 YEARS	12 YEARS
50	4 35	2 27	1 57	1 23	1 02	78	71	61	55
100	8 70	4 53	3 14	2 45	2 03	1 56	1 42	1 22	1 09
200	17 40	9 05	6 27	4 89	4 06	3 12	2 83	2 43	2 17
300	26 10	13 57	9 41	7 33	6 09	4 68	4 25	3 64	3 25
400	34 80	18 10	12 54	9 77	8 12	6 24	5 66	4 86	4 33
500	43 50	22 62	15 67	12 21	10 14	7 80	7 07	6 07	5 42
600	52 20	27 14	18 81	14 65	12 17	9 36	8 49	7 28	6 50
700	60 90	31 66	21 94	17 09	14 20	10 92	9 90	8 50	7 58
800	69 60	36 19	25 07	19 54	16 23	12 47	11 31	9 71	8 66
900	78 29	40 71	28 21	21 98	18 25	14 03	12 73	10 92	9 75
1000	86 99	45 23	31 34	24 42	20 28	15 59	14 14	12 14	10 83
2000	173 98	90 46	62 68	48 83	40 56	31 18	28 27	24 27	21 65
3000	260 97	135 69	94 01	73 24	60 83	46 76	42 42	36 40	32 48
4000	347 96	180 91	125 35	97 66	81 11	62 35	56 55	48 54	43 30
5000	434 95	226 14	156 69	122 07	101 39	77 94	70 69	60 67	54 13
6000	521 94	271 37	188 02	146 48	121 66	93 52	84 83	72 80	64 95
7000	608 92	316 60	219 36	170 90	141 94	109 11	98 96	84 93	75 78
8000	695 91	361 82	250 70	195 31	162 22	124 69	113 10	97 07	86 60
9000	782 90	407 05	282 03	219 72	182 49	140 28	127 24	109 20	97 43
10000	869 89	452 28	313 37	244 13	202 77	155 87	141 37	121 33	108 25
15000	1304 83	678 41	470 05	366 20	304 15	233 80	212 06	182 00	162 37
20000	1739 77	904 55	626 73	488 26	405 53	311 73	282 74	242 66	216 50
25000	2174 72	1130 69	783 41	610 33	506 91	389 66	353 42	303 32	270 62
30000	2609 66	1356 82	940 10	732 39	608 30	467 59	424 11	363 99	324 74
35000	3044 60	1582 96	1096 78	854 46	709 68	545 52	494 79	424 65	378 86
40000	3479 54	1809 10	1253 46	976 52	811 06	623 45	565 47	485 32	432 99
45000	3914 48	2035 23	1410 14	1098 59	912 44	701 38	636 16	545 98	487 11
46000	4001 47	2080 46	1441 48	1123 00	932 72	716 97	650 29	558 11	497 93
47000	4088 46	2125 69	1472 81	1147 41	953 00	732 56	664 43	570 24	508 76
48000	4175 45	2170 91	1504 15	1171 83	973 27	748 14	678 57	582 38	519 58
49000	4262 44	2216 14	1535 49	1196 24	993 55	763 33	692 70	594 51	530 41
50000	4349 43	2261 37	1566 82	1220 65	1013 82	779 32	706 84	606 64	541 23
51000	4436 41	2306 60	1598 16	1245 06	1034 10	794 90	720 98	618 78	552 06
52000	4523 40	2351 82	1629 50	1269 48	1054 38	810 49	735 11	630 91	562 88
53000	4610 39	2397 05	1660 83	1293 89	1074 65	826 07	749 25	643 04	573 70
54000	4697 38	2442 28	1692 17	1318 30	1094 93	841 66	763 39	655 17	584 53
55000	4784 37	2487 51	1723 51	1342 72	1115 21	857 25	777 52	667 31	595 35
56000	4871 36	2532 73	1754 84	1367 13	1135 48	872 83	791 66	679 44	606 18
57000	4958 35	2577 96	1786 18	1391 54	1155 76	888 42	805 80	691 57	617 00
58000	5045 33	2623 19	1817 51	1415 95	1176 04	904 01	819 93	703 71	627 83
59000	5132 32	2668 42	1848 85	1440 37	1196 31	919 59	834 07	715 84	638 65
60000	5219 31	2713 64	1880 19	1464 78	1216 59	935 18	848 21	727 97	649 48
61000	5306 30	2758 87	1911 52	1489 19	1236 87	950 76	862 34	740 10	660 30
62000	5393 29	2804 10	1942 86	1513 61	1257 14	966 35	876 48	752 24	671 13
63000	5480 28	2849 32	1974 20	1538 02	1277 42	981 94	890 62	764 37	681 95
64000	5567 26	2894 55	2005 53	1562 43	1297 69	997 52	904 75	776 50	692 77
65000	5654 25	2939 78	2036 87	1586 84	1317 97	1013 11	918 89	788 63	703 60
67500	5871 72	3052 85	2115 21	1647 88	1368 66	1052 07	954 23	818 97	730 66
70000	6089 20	3165 92	2193 55	1708 91	1419 35	1091 04	989 57	849 30	757 72
75000	6524 14	3392 05	2350 23	1830 97	1520 73	1168 97	1060 26	909 96	811 84
80000	6959 08	3618 19	2506 91	1953 04	1622 12	1246 90	1130 94	970 63	865 97
85000	7394 02	3844 32	2663 60	2075 10	1723 50	1324 83	1201 62	1031 29	920 09
90000	7828 96	4070 46	2820 28	2197 17	1824 88	1402 76	1272 31	1091 95	974 21
95000	8263 91	4296 60	2976 96	2319 23	1926 26	1480 70	1342 99	1152 62	1028 33
100000	8698 85	4522 73	3133 64	2441 30	2027 64	1558 63	1413 67	1213 28	1082 46
105000	9133 79	4748 87	3290 32	2563 36	2128 03	1636 56	1484 36	1273 94	1136 58
110000	9568 73	4975 01	3447 01	2685 43	2230 41	1714 49	1555 04	1334 61	1190 70
115000	10003 67	5201 14	3603 69	2807 49	2331 79	1792 42	1625 72	1395 27	1244 83
120000	10438 62	5427 28	3760 37	2929 56	2433 17	1870 35	1696 41	1455 94	1298 95
125000	10873 56	5653 42	3917 05	3051 62	2534 55	1948 28	1767 09	1516 60	1353 07
130000	11308 50	5879 55	4073 73	3173 68	2635 94	2026 21	1837 77	1577 26	1407 18
135000	11743 44	6105 69	4230 41	3295 75	2737 32	2104 14	1908 46	1637 93	1461 32
140000	12178 38	6331 83	4387 10	3417 81	2838 70	2182 08	1979 14	1698 59	1515 44
145000	12613 33	6557 96	4543 78	3539 88	2940 08	2260 01	2049 82	1759 26	1569 56
150000	13048 27	6784 10	4700 46	3661 94	3041 46	2337 94	2120 51	1819 92	1623 68

103

NECESSARY TO AMORTIZE A LOAN

AMOUNT	15 YEARS	18 YEARS	20 YEARS	25 YEARS	28 YEARS	29 YEARS	30 YEARS	35 YEARS	40 YEARS
50	48	44	42	39	38	37	37	38	35
100	96	88	84	78	75	74	74	72	70
200	192	175	168	155	150	148	147	143	140
300	287	263	251	232	225	222	221	214	209
400	383	350	335	309	299	296	294	285	279
500	478	438	419	386	374	370	367	356	348
600	574	525	502	464	449	444	441	427	418
700	669	613	586	541	523	518	514	498	487
800	765	700	670	618	598	592	588	569	557
900	861	788	753	695	673	666	661	640	626
1000	9 58	8 75	8 37	7 72	7 47	7 40	7 34	7 11	6 96
2000	19 12	17 50	16 73	15 44	14 94	14 80	14 68	14 21	13 91
3000	28 67	26 25	25 10	23 16	22 41	22 20	22 02	21 37	20 86
4000	38 23	35 00	33 46	30 88	29 88	29 60	29 36	28 42	27 82
5000	47 79	43 75	41 83	38 60	37 34	37 00	36 69	35 52	34 77
6000	57 34	52 50	50 19	46 31	44 81	44 40	44 03	42 62	41 72
7000	66 90	61 25	58 56	54 03	52 28	51 80	51 37	49 72	48 68
8000	76 46	70 00	66 92	61 75	59 75	59 20	58 71	56 83	55 63
9000	86 01	78 75	75 28	69 47	67 21	66 60	66 04	63 93	62 58
10000	95 57	87 50	83 65	77 19	74 68	74 00	73 38	71 03	69 54
15000	143 35	131 25	125 47	115 78	112 02	111 00	110 07	106 54	104 30
20000	191 14	175 00	167 29	154 37	149 36	147 99	146 76	142 06	139 07
25000	238 92	218 75	209 12	192 96	186 69	184 99	183 45	177 57	173 83
30000	286 70	262 49	250 94	231 55	224 03	221 99	220 13	213 08	208 60
35000	334 48	306 24	292 76	270 14	261 37	258 99	256 82	248 60	243 36
40000	382 27	349 99	334 58	308 73	298 71	295 98	293 51	284 11	278 13
45000	430 05	393 74	376 40	347 32	336 05	332 98	330 20	319 62	312 90
46000	439 60	402 49	384 77	355 04	343 51	340 38	337 54	326 73	319 85
47000	449 16	411 24	393 13	362 76	350 98	347 78	344 87	333 83	326 80
48000	458 72	419 99	401 50	370 48	358 45	355 18	352 21	340 93	333 75
49000	468 27	428 74	409 86	378 19	365 92	362 58	359 55	348 03	340 71
50000	477 83	437 49	418 23	385 91	373 38	369 98	366 89	355 14	347 66
51000	487 39	445 24	426 59	393 63	380 85	377 38	374 22	362 24	354 61
52000	496 94	454 99	434 95	401 35	388 32	384 78	381 56	369 34	361 57
53000	506 50	462 74	443 32	409 07	395 79	392 18	388 90	376 44	368 52
54000	516 06	472 48	451 68	416 78	403 25	399 58	396 24	383 55	375 47
55000	525 61	481 23	460 05	424 50	410 72	406 98	403 59	390 65	382 43
56000	535 17	489 98	468 41	432 22	418 19	414 37	410 91	397 75	389 38
57000	544 73	498 73	476 78	439 94	425 66	421 77	418 25	404 85	396 33
58000	554 28	507 48	485 14	447 66	433 13	429 17	425 59	411 96	403 29
59000	563 84	516 23	493 50	455 38	440 59	436 57	432 93	419 06	410 24
60000	573 40	524 98	501 87	463 09	448 06	443 97	440 26	426 16	417 19
61000	582 95	533 73	510 23	470 81	455 53	451 37	447 60	433 26	424 15
62000	592 51	542 48	518 60	478 53	463 00	458 77	454 94	440 37	431 10
63000	602 07	551 23	526 96	486 25	470 48	466 17	462 28	447 47	438 05
64000	611 62	559 98	535 33	493 97	477 83	473 57	469 61	454 57	445 00
65000	621 18	568 73	543 69	501 68	485 40	480 97	476 95	461 67	451 96
67000	645 07	590 60	564 60	520 98	504 07	499 47	495 30	479 43	469 34
70000	668 96	612 48	585 51	540 28	522 74	517 97	513 64	497 19	486 72
75000	716 74	656 23	627 34	578 87	560 07	554 96	550 33	532 70	521 49
80000	764 53	699 98	669 16	617 48	597 41	591 96	587 02	568 21	556 25
85000	812 31	743 72	710 98	656 05	634 75	628 96	623 70	603 73	591 02
90000	860 09	787 47	752 80	694 64	672 09	665 96	660 39	639 24	625 79
95000	907 87	831 22	794 62	733 23	709 43	702 95	697 08	674 75	660 55
100000	955 66	874 97	836 45	771 82	746 76	739 95	733 77	710 27	695 32
105000	1003 44	918 72	878 27	810 41	784 10	776 95	770 46	745 78	730 08
110000	1051 22	962 46	920 09	849 00	821 44	813 95	807 15	781 29	764 85
115000	1099 00	1006 21	961 91	887 59	858 78	850 94	843 83	816 81	799 61
120000	1146 79	1049 96	1003 73	926 18	896 12	887 94	880 52	852 32	834 38
125000	1194 57	1093 71	1045 56	964 78	933 45	924 94	917 21	887 83	869 14
130000	1242 35	1137 46	1087 38	1003 37	970 79	961 93	953 90	923 34	903 91
135000	1290 14	1181 20	1129 20	1041 96	1008 13	998 93	990 59	958 86	938 68
140000	1337 92	1224 95	1171 02	1080 55	1045 47	1035 93	1027 28	994 37	973 44
145000	1385 70	1268 70	1212 84	1119 14	1082 81	1072 93	1063 96	1029 88	1008 21
150000	1433 48	1312 45	1254 67	1157 73	1120 14	1109 92	1100 65	1065 40	1042 97

BUYING A FORECLOSURE HOME

There are many people out there that are looking to purchase a foreclosure home. Nothing is wrong with buying foreclosures. Even if you could get one, there are different ways that you can approach a foreclosure. You could go to the foreclosure auction when they are being conducted most time at your country court house or where-ever they may have them in your area. If you are not sure you could ask your realtor, there is the possibility he or she will help you.

The bad thing about this foreclosure auction is, you virtually have to have all the cash money. Surprising, isn't it? Now, once you plan to go to the auction you should have an idea of the price of the home you intend to purchase or bid on. When you go to the auction you will be required to deposit 10% of the amount of the selling price. The bad thing is, if you are looking to put down 3% or 5% then you should know this, auction is not for you, worst of all is you will have to come up with the rest of money in thirty days, so you will have to make sure that money will be available to you in 30 days.

Let's look on what actually happen when you go to an auction to bid on a home for $100,000. Going to the sale would require for you to have $10,000 in cash, bank check, money orders or certified checks. This amount represents 10% of the selling price. The remaining amount of money you will have left to pay on this offer would be $90,000. This $90,000 would become due and payable thirty days after you have made the 10% deposit, now before you make the deposit of 10%, it has to be very clear where, when, and how the other $90,000 will be in your hand. You might not believe it, but if you did not come up with the $90,000 within the time specified you stand the chance of losing your deposit of $10,000.

There is no such thing as making the deposit, and then going to look for the money, that is too risky, you should not do that, you should know where the money is coming from or better yet, if you have it into your possession, it would be better. These are precautionary steps that you are getting; there are some chances you do not take. If it is looking risky, then don't do it.

Another way to look into foreclosures are, if you get the list of foreclosures, you could go to the home of the homeowner and be polite about it, let the family know that you are very sorry, but you have learned their home might be foreclosing, and you would like to assist them by buying their home before it's foreclosed. Tell them if you buy their home before the auction, it would save their credit, and would get them some money to start anew. If the foreclosure takes place, they will probably get nothing, and their credit would be tarnished. Once the home owner accepts your buying their home, you can negotiate with the owner of the home. In this case, you have more time at your hand to do a 3or 5% down and go to a lending institution to secure a mortgage for the purchase. Negotiating with the seller, can get you more time than going to an auction. Best wishes on your foreclosure search.

HOW TO PURCHASE WITH LITTLE OR NO MONEY

How to purchase with little or no money is what everyone likes to hear, and not only to hear but to do. Your goal is to buy real estate, but you have very limited amount of money, and no knowledge of how much down payment you really need. I think I have already emphasized what the down payment is. It is the money you give to your attorney when you go to sign the contract.

The down payment is also known as the money you put up at contract to show the seller you intend to purchase his or her home. You show good faith by putting down that deposit. Now what happen if you do not have that deposit check to put down, how can you show good faith that you want to purchase the home? Now you have to learn how to incorporate some creativity and put the creativity to work. This is where the skill of a real estate agent comes into play.

Before you make any move, talk with the seller let him know what you are trying to do, find out the position that the seller is in. If he is an anxious seller, he may just be tired of the property and want to get rid of it. Find out how long the property is on the market, if for a long time he will be willing to talk to all interested persons. Another thing is to find out how many people own the property, if it is one person it might be easier to negotiate with one than it is for two or more. The more people that own the property the harder it will be to negotiate. When you get all this information you are in a very good position to start your negotiation.

It is better to put no money down on a multiple family home. Why multiple family? In the first place, you do not have a lot of money to make a deposit, so my feeling tells me you would not have the money to make timely payments on a one family, but if you go after a two or three, you would be buying a gold mine, and not an alligator (where one sit and eats and get nothing out of it) although it will depend on the price you are paying for the property. Once you get in possession of this property, the following month there will rent to collect, so instead of you putting in money from your pocket that first month, you would be collecting rent. Powerful move, isn't it?

Now what you need to do is to find out the value of the property. Say the property worth is $150,000 negotiate with the seller, maybe the property is what you call a "no wanting." This means the owner is there but he or she really do not care about the property and is just waiting for you to mention the word sale. He is waiting to make any kind of a deal while he gets some money to walk away with. It is possible they will hold the down payment, again ask for what you want, it is just possible you may get it. Another good way to look on this is to find out the type of mortgage the property has on it. You need to know this, for if they have what is called an assumable mortgage tell you what, if it is, you should go right ahead and take advantage of the opportunity, that would be money in your pocket. This type of assumable mortgages is the best, if the rates are good. If the rates are above the going rates, then you might want to think again before you take on the assumable loan. There are variables, so you might want to look on the numbers carefully. It could be very inexpensive for you, there are some points that will be over looked. There are options that you have, so why not use the ones that are available. Nothing is wrong with asking, therefore, shame on you if you do not ask.

SHOULD I BUY A HANDYMAN SPECIAL?

What is a handyman special? There are many times I have gotten calls asking, about a handyman special? You see the real estate business is so complicated that we need interpreters for many things. A handyman special is simply a home that is in need of repairs, which means this property will not sell for its normal price because of its present condition. Sometimes the homes need severe work while others may just need minor work, again, what is major for you might be minor for others. If you do not understand the difference between major and minor work ask an expert in that area of work. No one would tell you not to buy a handyman special, because that could be your bread and butter and you do not know it. You could buy a handyman special, put little money in the fixing of it and resell it in a short time and make a good profit. There is nothing wrong with that as it is quite legal. There are many people doing that who are making a comfortable living doing it, you can do the same. I hope you will stop thinking about it and do it after you have read my book. The advantages are there, explore them and you will be successful. It is always good to look at it from a worst-case scenario. Obviously, we would like the property to make us a lot of money, but the chances are there, that things might not work out the way in which we would like them to. The worst thing that can happen to you is that you are stuck with the property in its original state, but guess what, it still worth what you paid for it, although I have never seen this happen. There is always someone to make that purchase from you. There are things that could derail the sale for a while but if you try to find what is stopping the sale and correct it, the sale will go through. If there is a price barrier it is as simple as reducing the price. There is one thing that cannot be done and is to relocate the property. Other factors can be corrected or controlled.

HOW DO I FIND FORECLOSURES

Finding foreclosures are not hard, what is hard is to get them. Sometimes we see foreclosures for sale in the newspapers. If you buy and search the classified section of the paper, there you will find all types of property for sale including foreclosures. From there you could go ahead in making the necessary steps to acquire whatever might be of interest to you. It has been your dream years and the possibilities are there, you are free to explore them.

Another way of finding foreclosures is to visit your town hall. When you go there the first time you might not understand how to find list of foreclosures, but you could kindly ask someone that work there to assist you. Once you are being helped, ask question so the next time you can help yourself. The next time around, the third place to look for these deals is at your county court house. Again, you will need help for the first time, but once you learn you are on your way. These are some of the best ways to butter your bread and don't look over your shoulder.

There is another I did not tell you about, which is to drive to different neighborhoods. You can spot them as you see them. If you see a home that the roof is looking bad, around the home is bushy, and you see old newspapers on the steps, or stuck in the mail box what is that telling you, read between the lines. There is simply no one living there. What should I do, you may ask? It's for you to get to work try find the owner, ask the person living next door or better, write down the address of the property take it to your realtor, and ask him or her to check it out for you. They will be happy to do it. These are just some of the different steps you can take to find yourself a bargain. I think you should explore them. It is not as easy you might think, but it's certainly will worth every moment when you find the right bargain. Many people have overlooked the opportunities that are next door, or even in their back yard, you should, take action when the opportunities arise. Capitalize on the real estate market, it is not luck, but whosoever is willing to take the challenges.

I have seen many people sit by and watch others take challenges and became winners, then they attribute their success to luck. I believe it is better to do something than to do nothing. To do nothing is very easy, but it gets you nowhere. Why not take the challenges and become a winner?

There are many people that sit and speak of how broke they are, but when it comes to do something about how broke they are, they refused to take action. Oh, they are so afraid of doing something, for they might start doing things and make money, the worst of it they would not be broke any more, and that scares them. They are contented being broke, yet they complain. Folks, it is better to do something and get nothing, because the next time around you will learn how to do it differently to get a positive result. In the process you are learning. If you do nothing, your reward will be double zeros, or even triple. Some people are so lazy they consider it a crime, if they strife for the things that will help them to progress. In one of Paul's writings he said, "I will learn to be contented in what-ever state I am" but he later said,

"I will press to-wards the mark of the higher calling" this tells us that we should never be satisfied in our broke state.

ESTABLISHING A WORKING RELATIONSHIP

It is good for buyers and realtors to establish a working relationship on the first day they met. Buying a home is a process and not an event. Developing a good business relationship is good and will assure you the best of service and least amount of problems. When sellers place their homes in the hands of realtors, they are placing their trust in the hands of such realtor. The real estate company with all its agents and brokers form a team that work together to sell that property.

When a realtor sells a property, compensation for the listing agent is ensured through a listing contract. Commission is also paid to the realtor that actually sells the property. Another Realtor may bring in a buyer, through a sign in the yard read about it in the newspaper, or simply being told by a friend. The next way would be, if the property was listed on the multiple listing services, the other realtor would be able to get it from the said Service. It is very crucial to know that there are a variety of ways that listing agents can find buyers. It is imperative therefore that you have the right realtor.

Realtors take certain risk when they work with buyers without a listing contract to protect themselves. Realtors have only the trust and relationship to go on when they show buyers a home. In exchange for the buyers' loyalty, realtors provide professional assistance to buyers and facilitate a smooth transaction. A realtor relies on the buyer's loyalty before investing time and energy into pursuing a home that meets the needs of the buyers. While there are open houses, for sale by owners, and even cold calling may be used effectively to find the right home. The most common method realtor's use is the Multiple Listing Systems. Realtors share listing information through the (MLS) sellers gain maximum exposure to their properties by using this system. Whenever a home is listed for sale by a realtor, it is entered into the MLS system if the realtor is a member of the organization.

It is therefore important that when you are listing your home for sale, you tell the realtors that you would like your home to go on the MLS where it would get maximum exposure. There it could be viewed on the computer system and other places. There are some systems that allow realtors to enter their prospects search parameters in the computer, so that realtor can efficiently check day to day to see if any new properties have come on the market. Not only does the MLS system allows the buyers access to present sales, but past sold information that will educate them on the state of the market. It is usually through the MLS system that buyers find the right home. They could view the price range or location which is very important. My word of encouragement is, if at all you want to get anywhere in real estate you have to start and work your way to the top. Wait patiently for the right deal to come along. There is no need to be in a rush. I have proven this several times. A working relationship becomes mutual when both parties do what they have to do. If you tell the realtor what you want, I believe he will respect your request and do what you have asked while it is legal and is in the best interest of you the seller. When you visit your realtor, try and establish that working relationship whether you are a seller or a buyer.

HOW DO I SELL MY HOME

As they say, first impression counts, if you understand this notion it will help in selling your home. Selling and buying of real estate is what Realtors do best. Before your home goes on the market you should ask yourself one question such as, "am I ready to sell my home"? This is a very important decision you are making. I have seen sellers call realtors and put their homes on the market and after two days took the home off the market. This does not mean they got their prices but they were not sure what they wanted to do. Selling your home especially your primary residence has to be carefully thought out. It is a process that will affect you and your family therefore, you should be well informed. Once your home is sold, you have to move so there has to be a place secured for you to live. You might have to move in with a friend or relative. Whatever the case, bear in mind there must be a place to live. This might be surprising to say but I have to say it because it is true. I have seen on several occasions where sellers place their homes in contract for sale and do not think of where they will be living once the property is sold. Whether you are selling through an agent or yourself, the true reality is that you will have to move. Your move should be determined even before your home goes on the market. You should not be frightened by a signed contract because you have nowhere to live, "**stay ahead of the game**".

Many homeowners sold their property on their own! Sure, you can, although it is not an easy task. They might want to do this for different reasons, maybe they do not want to pay a commission to a broker for selling their home, or maybe they do not want their neighbors to have knowledge that they are selling their property. It is also possible they do not want to see a real estate agent coming to and from their home, or surprisingly, some sellers do not like real estate agents. There are many homeowners, who sell their property on their own, and sure you can too, no one is saying you cannot. When your home goes on the market, make sure that you are ready for the move.

There are some things to look into which could bring down the value of a property, you might not even know what they are and sometimes not even aware of what these minor things could do regarding the sale. Sometimes we know but take them for granted, because they are looking quite simply but are not. Selling your home is a process that will affect you and the decision you make, so stay informed. In order to get the price your home is worth you need someone with experience that you can trust. Selling the property, yourself does not mean you will pocket the commission. With an experience buyer, you may wind up putting less than the commission in your pocket, surprising, isn't it? You might not know but I am telling you the truth. An experience buyer knows how to negotiate, and could negotiate more than the commission into his or her pocket. When you do not know who your buyers are, the prudent thing to do is to seek an expert.

What about a qualified buyer, how do you find one? Sellers have to make sure they do not waste three months with an unqualified buyer. This could cost you more than you would necessarily spend with a qualified real estate professional. A good reason for working with an experience agent is, they have plenty of information at hand, and not only so, they have the source of getting their information. They are very careful in screening the potential buyers. They have given up valuable time to get the prudent information that are necessary for bringing a ready, willing, and able buyer to your home. You see, Realtors prefer not to waste time with a person who is out for a good evening and want to take a preview at properties, but hasn't decided it that the best way to go is through a to use a realtor. We try to avoid site seeing with buyers, if they want to do site seeing they would have to do it on their own by finding the property that says, "for sale by owner". By using this method, they could visit all the properties they want and in doing, so waste their time and you the sellers.

SOMETHING THAT WILL MAKE YOUR HOME SELL

Remember what first attracted you to your home when you bought it? What were the most appealing features? Now that you are selling you need to look at it as if you were buying it all over again. □ere are many times home owners place a sign in front of their home that reads "for sale by owner" I want to let you know that sometimes a sign alone cannot and will not sell your home. When your home goes on the market it is now competing with other homes that are on the market and needs just more than a sign in front of it. You want your home to sell in the shortest time possible, therefore, you should get all the exposure you possibly can for the sale and at the right price, which is why you should talk to a Realtor. I am not saying you cannot sell your property yourself, but there could be some disadvantages in trying to do it yourself. Your home has a for-sale sign in front of it, or in a window, will only be seen by those who pass by it, don't you need more exposure than that?

Secondly, you will be leaving yourself vulnerable to have too many people walking from the street into your home without knowing who they are; neither would you know if they are ready, willing and able to purchase your home. Don't take chances; it is better to pay a commission to a Realtor. In case you are in a state of shock because of this, I would like to share with you a few things other than a sign that will help sell your property. There are basically five things that you should take into consideration when selling.

- Pricing:

    If the price is right, there will always be a buyer. There are buyers all over the place; they walk the streets every day. They pass by your property by the minute. Although there is a sign that says "for sale", if the price is not right, they will ask and keep passing until you are tired and frustrated, then you will get the right price. When selling your home, the price you set is a critical factor in the response you'll receive.

    There are several factors that are based on the selling of the property.

- Terms have a role to play when selling.

    There are many buyers that want to buy with very little cash and even though they may have a good job, the cash might not be there. They are looking for someone to say, "I will hold the mortgage for you" or "I will carry a portion of your mortgage". That would be some incentive to the buyer and also bring about a faster sale, we call it a flexible seller. This can also put some extra money in the seller's pocket. Once you carry a mortgage on the sale, you are entitled to some kind of incentive, we call that interest. This could only be done if you the seller are not depending on the money from the sale to put you into another home.

Market condition; The market condition is the way the property should be presented when it is placed on the market. Sometimes the physical condition probably has to be change, or maybe it needs a coat of paint. If needs be, go ahead and make the necessary changes, so the property will become more marketable. Most times when a home goes on the market the seller might say, I sell as is, which is correct, the home can be sold in a "as is" condition. Here's what will happen, it may take longer to sell and you will get less money. If the home doesn't need much money to fix, you should go right ahead and do the minor work it needs making it better for you the seller. There are buyers that are looking for a home and don't know the price of a gallon of semi glass paint, or the difference between semi and flat. To that buyer it will seem like a whole lot of work and money to paint even one room, so you could see that if the house is painted, that individual will purchase the property for more, because a simple repair looks like a million-dollar project.

Let's look on location as the fourth-selling tool. We know that you cannot move the home, so the location has to be right. What you might need to do is to use some expensive paint to paint the home. Do little extra work to make up for the location since you cannot remove the property.

Put up a nice chandelier in the living room; use some inexpensive carpet to do the flooring. In this case, you have no control over the location but you do whatever you can to make the property become attractive and to bring about the sale. Once the buyer looks at the home and sees that it is well put together, it will to attract said buyer. You will be in for a faster sale, and even a higher price in a location that isn't necessary the best, but the condition of the home could bring a higher price.

Our fifth and final tool is exposure. We will agree that exposure is good for the sale of a property. It is possible that you could tell your friend, and he will tell another friend about the sale. That is a very slow process of exposure. You could also put up a sign before your home that "says for sale" as most people do these days. Some people go a little further by running an advertisement in the newspaper which is also good. There is another way of selling your property. This is called maximum exposure. You talk to your real estate broker next door. Ask him or her if they are a member of the multiple listing services (MLS). If you are not sure what MLS is, ask your broker and he or she will be glad to explain to you if you are going to list your property with their office. Once you list, they will give your home all the exposure there is. You could also ask the Realtor to take down your little cardboard sign you have on the window and replace it with a professional sign from his office. This type of exposure that your property will now receive will be phenomenal. You have worked hard for your home therefore you should do your best to preserve it, and to make sure you receive the maximum price. Some sellers put a little sign in the window that cannot be read from the street. If you want to read the sign, you would have to climb over a fence to read the little script on the board. These are reasons why you need to talk with a professional; he/she will help you to sell your home professionally and trust me, when you see all that he/she has to go through, you will agree that he/she is worthy of commission, because it is hard work.

THE BEST TIME TO SELL

There are many potential sellers who want to sell their homes but don't know what to do or when to take auction to sell. They sit in hopes for the sale to take place and in a short while they sit doing nothing, this is really true. Not very long ago, I went to show a property for sale. I showed the property and was walking away when the next-door neighbor saw me on my way out and called me. I was quite polite to him not knowing that he was the owner of the property. By talking to him he said, "you know I wanted to sell my home". That was exactly what I wanted to hear. I called that "good news to my ear" The following day I went and got the listing. A week later, his home was sold. The best time to sell your home is when you decide that you are ready to sell, whether you are going to move out of town or moving into a bigger or nicer home. You are the determining factor.

A good thing to do is to talk to a professional in the field. If you have no experience of marketing a property, don't feel bad, but shame on you if you don't call a professional. Although it is your home you may still need some advice. The more educated you are about selling the more chance there is to make more money. You should never be in a rush to sell. If you are in a rush, you will not have time to select the better buyer and that means you might lose money. You will be that eager to say yes to the first offer. Give yourself plenty of time,

126

more time means more money. My advice to you is, never be in a rush to sell your home. If you do, you are selling yourself short. It would be good for you to observe the market to see what way it is going, whether it is going up or down. Another factor that will affect the sale is the interest rate. When the rate is low there will be more buyers. Naturally, if the rate is high, people will look, but it will be hard to convert those lookers into buyers unless you can come up with a good deal as some people called it. As you know quite well, everyone in the market is looking for a deal, and so should you, if you could find one.

We know that the weather changes in some parts of the country and this makes the selling process as it were, seasonal. In those areas where the weather gets very cold and icy, there are homes that do not show too well because the ground might be covered with snow. People like to do their home shopping when the weather is pleasant and they can see the ground. Most sellers do not want to show their homes when the weather is bad. There might be too much traffic going to and from with all that water from their feet. No one likes that! Do you agree? We tend to believe that more homebuyers start their home shopping in early spring going through the summer into the early winter. If you intend to sell your home, why don't you make a little flower garden to the front of the home or by the side, this will make a big difference in the showing more than it would without the garden. Try it and look for the results.

MARKETING YOUR HOME

It is very important to take marketing in consideration. Look back a couple pages and you will get some inside tips about marketing your home. If you use the marketing technique, they should bring you success, and increase your profit margin. I think it might be hard to find any other kind of ways to improve your market strategies than what have been mentioned in this book. Of course, many people say they can sell their home in any condition. The only thing that is wrong is, you simply will not be able to get the price you probably wanted. It might stay on the market one year longer at an even a lower price. Putting a couple of dollars into minor repairs could give you a faster sale and twice the dollar amount it cost for that minor repair. There is nothing wrong in painting the home for the buyer, you will pick up a couple of dollars more.

I want to give you a little hint in regards to selling of your property try it and you will find out that it works. Before you place your home on the market with that for sale sign on it or into the window, take a walk-in front of the property and take a good look at it and see if there could be any type of improvement that could be made. This will make it look more presentable to the eye of the buyers. If there is anything that you have seen that could improve the property, don't let anyone tell you not to do it, just go ahead and do the improvement.

Once it is done, take another view of the property as you did before and compare both views. A better thing that you could do is to take a picture before you do the improvement and after, you will see the difference for yourself.

WHAT IF MY HOUSE DON'T SELL

Putting your home on the market for sale is a process. Your home being on the market for sale does not mean that you are guaranteed a fast sale. What will happen is, there will be a lot of calling about the home. If there is a for sale sign by the owner then he or she will also get lots of unwanted guests. This will go on for a limited time. What you will need to do is to notice when your calls are getting less and less per day, and the home is not sold. You might need to start asking yourself why my home is not sold after so many calls. You need to know what the problem is, so adjustments can be made where applicable. It's possible that the pricing of the property is too high. Maybe you should have done a little painting. It's possible that the fence needs repairing if there is one. You need to take a second look, so you could find where to make adjustments.

If you do not pause to find out why your property is not sold, it could be there until the sign becomes dead and is doing nothing but adding frustration to you and your home; then your property ends up as refusal and leave a bad taste to prospective buyers, wondering why the home hasn't been sold after a long period of time. Now, they are going to draw to conclusion that there must be something wrong why your home is not sold. You can sell your property yourself, but if you seek the help of a Realtor you will avoid costly mistakes and wasted time. You will agree that owning a home is your biggest investment that you can ever make, and you should try to take good care of it. This is why I said, when in dough, seek the advice of a professional it will do better than hurt in the process.

One simple mistake could cause you to lose the sale while trying to save the commission you think you are saving. After looking into all the possibilities and your home is not sold, you might have to do what no one would be happy doing. "You might have to reduce the price and do a little painting to review the property and place it back on the market.

Another way of selling is that some broker or investor will buy your home at a reduced price if it is not sold after a period of time. This might be your best chance after a long trial if you have to sell because of your job relocation, or you are just tired of being a city person. If there is no real rush for money you could even let someone know that you are willing to take back the mortgage. This could bring about a fast sale and more money to you as the seller. If you do not understand how this works you could ask your attorney to explain it to you.

HOW DO I PRICE MY HOUSE?

Everyone thinks their home is worth a whole lot of money, and their home is the best. But it does not matter how you think, and what you think, it just will not sell for what you think. You may say "oh" I have just put a new boiler, or I just did the roof. That is alright, for the home would not sell without a boiler unless you are selling at a reduced price, the same goes for the roof, and you know what your home would be called a "handyman special"

Before you sell, consult a professional, he or she will help you with the pricing. Pricing has to do with the condition of your home. The location might not be a factor in some cases, while in other ways location can affect the sale. If the location is not desirable, then you might have to use the price to sweeten the sale. Many times, it will be your next-door neighbors' home that was sold recently. If the home was priced right, it will help to bring about a good price for your home. If it was sold by a professional, someone that knows the market and probably did a (C.M.A) comparable market analysis for that home it would definitely do well for you. The CMA will show all the homes that were sold within a certain radius of your property that is similar to yours; this could generate more money for you. Whatever you do, it is important to consult a real estate specialist to assist you in your real estate transaction.

This will help you to get a fair market value for your home. A good realtor has a dual role to play in the industry, you will not go wrong dealing with an experienced agent.

WHAT IS A FAIR MARKET VALUE?

Most buyers always ask a little more that they would normally be looking for or what they know the market can bear. Everyone wants more, and more, so they leave room for negotiation. It is normally through negotiating that they reach an agreement with the seller. In most cases the agent would do a comparable market analysis and may increase the price say five percent or so for negotiation, in most cases five percent markup on the price. This would give a fair market value of the property. You may even want to consult a real estate appraisal that would also do a CMA for your home. If you are in a rush and want a quick sale, you may think the suggested price is reasonable. Other- wise you may think it's not. What would you pay for the property if you were the buyer? You have to decide on a price that you feel is competitive, and is consistent with what other homes in your area have sold for. It is possible that you may get a couple of thousand more or less, depending upon the immediate condition of the property. This is why it is good to keep your home in good condition so that when you are ready to sell, there will not be too much repairs. If there are many repairs, you may have to lower your price or you may have to market your property as a handyman special. That means, "Less money"

A handyman special is a home that is on the market for sale that needs work, with the expectation that the buyer will buy, and do the work. Some people call it a fix upper which is the same as a handyman special; it is just a choice of words. Whatever term is used it means your home needs work. This type of property would not be sold for a regular price. You the seller would not be able to demand the price you would like to and should be taken in account before even putting the home on the market. Fair market value is what the property is worth based upon its condition, and the type of market we are in at the time of sale.

SHOULD I FIX MY HOUSE BEFORE I SELL IT?

Selling your home is an involved process that has to do with the biggest investment that can ever be made in a life time, and should be carefully thought of. It is alright to fix up your home before it goes on the market. There is no law to say that you have to fix, or you do not have to fix. It is just a matter of the kind of money you are expecting to come out of the sale with. If you fix the property, you will make more money versus you not doing the necessary repairs. What is required here is simple logic. If the property is in good condition, you will be able to demand more money for it. There will be more prospective buyers and you will agree that you will have more people looking, which increase the chance of having a faster sale and a higher price in a shorter time. So, if you have the money to put into the property by way of fixing, do it.

Isn't it much easier to sell a home in good condition than that of a handyman? For most people they will not buy a handy man. They often times look on the effort of restoring the property as a tremendous amount of work and would not want to get involved. Some people have no idea of what it will take to restore a home in terms of material cost and labor. I am suggesting that if you are such a person, consult someone that has the knowledge of the work that needs to be done.

While the home is a handyman, there is plenty of room for negotiation if your home is fairly new or in good condition. Chances are, you might not need to do any work to get it ready for the market. The type of work depends upon the price you are asking. It would be good to do some outside work. This makes the property appealing and more buyers would want to see the inside.

Once the home is looking good on the outside it is going to entice prospective buyers, 98 percent of the time the home will sell faster at a higher price than expected. Sometimes you are passing a property and from the looks of the outside, you will say to yourself "that home looks good", isn't it true? I have said it myself and even to my friends on many occasions that I love to see a well-kept home. Although the home is not for sale, you are ready to purchase it. I have heard many people said, "if that home was for sale, I would buy it now" you might even say it yourself. So, it is good to fix the property before it goes on the market. You will agree that an outside appeal will generate some traffic. Although that will not be the only way in which you will be getting prospective buyers to see your home. If you list with the right realtor, he or she will give your home the full market exposure until it is sold. That is the way in which buyers will find your home. There are sellers that will call real estate agents and inform them of a home for sale, some will just say, I want my home sold because I have to get out of here soon, but you know what, "I do not want a lot of trafficking in my home" and please do not put up a sign on the property. It is possible to sell your home under these conditions, but it does not always work. This will have to do with market condition and price. In most cases, a realtor will need time to secure a willing and able buyer.

WHAT WILL MAKE MY HOUSE SELL

There is not just one thing that will make your home sell. There are different things that might have to go into a home to cause it to sell on a timely basis. Pricing will definitely play a role in the sale of your home. There is no question about that. If the home is priced below market value, there will be no other magic needed to sell it. If you are willing to do the necessary repairs needed including panting, your home will sell. One must remember that when we talk about painting is not just any kind of that paint can be used to make your home saleable. Some paint will of course turn off the buyer. I remember shopping for a home once. I looked on the home that was freshly painted, so you would think this home was marketable. Several people looked at the property and walked away from it yet it was freshly painted. No doubt you spend a good deal of time preparing the home for the market, but you did not do a good job, therefore, your effort became worthless.

Preparing your home for the market takes careful planning. You will have to capture the buyer's attention when he looks at your home. You would like the realtor to focus on the goal of selling your home, so you should give him the edge of doing so by giving the property that face lift it needs. If there are reasonable numbers of showings that are made to the property, and after 15 or 20 showings, there is not a buyer, this indicates that the home has got good market exposure but the price probably is high or the condition of the home was not good. In this case, corrective measures should be taken in the form of price reduction or some minor repairs. If corrective action can be taken, do not hesitate to do so. It could be a good idea to ask the prospective buyers what they like about the property, and what they did not like. This would give the seller a bit more edge if he knows the problem why the home was not sold. If the price of the property is the problem, then a price reduction is needed. These procedures will bring about the sale needed to complete the sale and prevent a nightmare.

REACHING PROSPECTIVE BUYERS

There is no one way of reaching prospective buyers, it's very important to use all the system available, to explore the market, if it is even by advertising. There was a time when selling a home was easy, but it's not any more. Some people plant a sign in front of their home or stick a piece of cardboard in the window that says "house for sale by owner". They might even go one step further and place an ad in the daily newspaper, and then wait hoping for the best. Of course, real estate agents do their thing too, but they will do a little more than what you the homeowner will do.

Agents take advantage of the MLS (Multiple Listing Services). The MLS system is very helpful. It helps to sell your property across town. The listing agent will place your home into the MLS system. The network would allow other brokers across town to have access to that listing. Also, real estate agents are in touch with buyers and sellers every day. They know the market and can reach buyers in most cases. I remembered talking to a lady, she told me that she wanted to sell her home. She had shown the property to so many people but no one showed interest in the property. I asked her to list the home with the company I work for, she said she don't want to, so I left her. One year after I asked her if her home was sold, she replied no. I ask her why was the home not sold after a year and if she was not interested in selling her home? yes, she answered. Why don't you give it to me I asked again? "It seems as if I have to do so now" she said. "When can I come over" I asked her, "tomorrow evening", she replied oh yes. That afternoon I went to the home and she gave me the listing. Now that I got the listing, the following day I made an appointment to show the home, she was looking a bit surprised, but she told me she was very happy when I called to show the property. I got an accepted offer, two days after I got the property listed, there was a contract of sale.

What happens is, agents have buyers that are ready to buy and in is most cases they need to get the listing, because they have the buyers waiting. Listing with an agent can bring about a faster sale and a higher price.

SHOWING YOUR HOUSE TO PROSPECTIVE BUYER

Showing your property to a prospective buyer should be done in a timely and orderly manner. Many people will think that there is no right procedure in showing their home. It is best to show the inside of the home first. Once you are finished looking on the outside, then it's time to walk away. You do not know what a buyer looks like so you have to show it to everyone and pay the same respect to all. Never take for granted that this person cannot buy a home, because of the way he or she dresses or the way they look. Buyers do not come in shapes, color or form.

I remember some years ago I was looking for a home, I walked unto the property where a developer was building homes for sale, I asked for the owner, he came to me and shouted, "I do not have any work". I was a bit surprised; I did not ask for a job, but he thought I could be there only for a job. He had the wrong concept of me not being able to purchase a home. Of my years in real estate, I have not seen buyers come in a special shape neither do they wear some special clothing. When I made mention of purchasing a home, he wanted to know if I had money for purchasing the property. We cannot be too careful of the way we treat prospective buyers. When I asked him not to get overly hung up with my looks or appearance and that I am a genuine buyer, he got a little bit surprised. My point is, everyone should be given the same treatment, opportunity and respect until proven otherwise. This man was building homes for sale, but he thought his buyers would be coming dressed in suites and driving one of the latest model cars. This is a wrong concept that should not be used. Finally, he had a change of heart and decided he was going to waste his time by showing me the property and so he did. He showed me four homes and after looking on the last one, I picked two which I purchased. He was out of his breath for a while, not one but two. He again looked at me and ask, where are you going to get money to buy two homes? My reply was "sir I will see you tomorrow." The following day I went back, made the necessary arrangements, took the paper work to the bank and purchase the two homes.

You never can say of any special ways that buyers do come. Whatever is done for one should be the same for all. Before you start showing your home, pick up all tools and store them in a store room, put all cans in the garbage, and close the door. Park your car on the street. Turn on the lights in the home, make up all the beds. It will give the home a different view, spray some air freshener in the home so it will smell fresh. There might be blown bulbs, replace them before you show the home. It will be good if you clean the stove, the refrigerator, if the faucets are leaking replace them, these are very important hints that will help you sell the property much faster. Some buyers think they are smart, of which they are, but because you are the buyer, and it is your money that you are spending you want to show them that you are smart. Make sure you keep it that way. They will say I have the money, it's true. I have to make sure I am happy with what I buy, that is true also. But sellers if you see the faults before it would be easier for you. When a buyer comes to your home, they will see that you are smarter. Some buyers are smart, they walk with a writing pad and pencil when they go to view a home. You will see they walk around they make notes. They are not saying what they are writing; you can only think that this is a smart buyer. He is making a list of different things could be done to improve the property. This is what you want them to do, because the home is in is in good condition so, the more you do before they come to view, the less they will have to write. The least they write, the better your chance of selling. When they cannot find what to write, then there is no excuse to buy. You have to get on top, and stay there. This type of marketing tactics will get you your price in a shorter time.

WHEN DO I START LOOKING FOR A HOME?

The best time to begin looking for a house is when you have fully decided what you want. You know how many bedrooms. The type of home you really want to live in, and if location is a factor, then you look for your location, and then all the different features you really want in you. Buying your first home is like having your first dream come through, you dream for a better quality of life therefore you have to plan for it. Your home might be a cozy starter or a sparkling mansion, you are making a life decision which reflects your personal needs and wants. If you do not decide and have a clear view in mind, you should withdraw yourself from the buying process until it clears in tour mind. you are setting up yourself for a big surprised and lot of wasted time, without even realizing. It is for you to know what you are looking for in a home, so you could go right into your home shopping. There are some buyers that as they see the home from the outside, they already know that is their home in this case you will avoid a lot of confusion in your shopping. It would certainly be a new definition of home shopping. Once you decide on the home, you are going to meet with your real estate broker. In the process of sitting with him or her you should be able to describe your home. You might need to make a little adjustment after talking with your broker, if so, that is alright, because in most cases you do not find the ideal property as you are looking for. Doing a little research on your own can be helpful, nothing is wrong with that. May be your neighbor or a friend already brought his or her home and is very happy with the purchase. You see, they might be able to educate you about your intention of purchasing, when you get these little tips before you meet with your agent, he will be more alert and careful when he talks to you. An educated consumer is the best to deal with. Whenever you start looking for a home you have to be aware that you are now a ready willing and able to buyer. This means you have what is known as earnest money deposited in the bank, not at home. The bank does not want to see that lump some of cash. You will have to satisfy the lending institution of how you get this money, before they agree to give you a loan. Being ready also means when you see the home that you like, you are going to do what is necessary to enter into a contract. This will show your willingness, and how able you are to complete the sale. The more knowledgeable you are, the better your final decision is likely to be. This handbook should serve as a door opener to those of you who are in the market to purchase a home. It should be a perfect fit for many individuals, because it lends itself to the buyers as well as the sellers.

DO I NEED A LAWYER WHEN PURCHASING A HOME?

Buying a home can be very complex and confusing process therefore you need an Attorney. There are some people that might be able to go through without an attorney, but as for you that are not versed with the different process and stages it is recommended that you use an attorney. There are legal papers that need to be drawn up and these are sometimes confusing and need an experienced Attorney. Your attorney will even accompany you to the closing to make sure it goes through as smoothly as possible. Not all attorneys' handle real estate transactions, so ask your agent for an attorney that will help you in your transaction. Never try to do it yourself, doing it yourself is when the closing is over and you are home, then you could do it yourself. By trying to save money, it could cause you more than you could even imagine. This is why we encourage you to use the expert. There are many of Attorneys out there, if you do not know one ask your agent, agents know plenty of real estate Attorneys and they will look out for you into the closing, and even after the closing is over. I knew a purchaser that was buying a home, when I ask him who his Attorney was, he replied that he did not need an Attorney, when I happen to find out his reason for not wanting to use an Attorney it was "they charge too much" so he obviously did not want to spend whatever the fees were to safe guard his investment. If you should stop to think for a while, the Attorney save you the purchaser a lot more money than what you really pay him.

HOW DO I FIND THE BEST BARGAIN?

In the real estate market, everyone is looking for a bargain, and nothing is wrong with finding a bargain. You might just have to wait until you find it, or, if you are fortunate, it might just come along your way. There is no escape, if you have patience and look hard enough, you will find one of the best real estate bargains around. Real estate is expensive and it is your biggest investment for your hard earn money, therefore, you should use lots of patience to preserve that which have worked so hard for. You are about to invest all that hard-earned money you have saved over the years; you should take a little time to spend it wisely. Look around for the home you want, not just look, but also tell a friend you are in the market of buying a home, they might want to sell, or have a friend that want to get rid of his or her home. There is nothing wrong with putting a little ad in your local newspaper. There might be a desperate seller reading the newspaper, there you will find your perfect match. There is a phrase that said "walk for nothing is better than sitting down." There are times you might just happen to be walking down the block and might notice a sign on a property that read for sale by owner, or you might see a home that is not properly taken care of. The yard might have high grass, there might be several newspapers on the stairs, some of the papers might even be burnt out by the sun, because they are there for a long time. Why not pass back in the evening when you know the lights should be on, if there is no light, that could be a good indicator. That could be your home, if you do not know how to go about it, contact your nearest realtor the following day and give the agent the information you know about the property, it is possible that two more or even ten more smart and well-informed prospective homebuyers have been reading my book, so do not delay if for any reason there is interest in the property. If you shop for a home this way, you can get a great bargain, while there are other ways you can do It also, but it might be a little more complicated. You could go to your town hall and do some research, but take my word for it, that might be too much work. If you contact your realtor, they do a faster job, because they already have the knowledge, and are more equipped to do the search at a much faster pace than your experimentations. Not all of us have learned, or and know how to use the internet, so many of us will have to go the old route, they are there, so why not take advantage of the opportunities that lay waste, they are there waiting for you to capitalize on them. If you are afraid, stand by and watch, someone is going to do it for you. The days of manner falling in our heads are over, these are the days of go get it, or stand there and perish, even if you have to do some wild goose chasing for what you want, so what? That is what many of us had to do to make stride. Good luck on your search, let me know how well you did. Let the days of looking for an apartment be history, start looking for bargains. No one is promising anything, we are saying that life owes to every man a living, and we want everyone to go out there and find what life has to offer you. There are times you may have to ask yourself the question, where do I go from here? If you are a believe you might say, "take my hand precious lord and lead me" for I cannot find the way without you. There are pains, aggravations, which can be very time consuming and is very costly in finding a place to live, so I want you to get out there and find your own. Many people do not think of the coast of moving as extra spending but it is. When you have your own home, it brings an amount of independency. You feel you are the man of your castle, what better feelings to have? Purchasing gives peace of mind, while pay your mortgage taxes, and insurance, (1) you are paying to yourself, no one will ever tell you to leave, or give an eviction notice unless your mortgage is not paid. (2) Insurance gives peace of mind, in case there is a disaster of any kind, there would be some compensation to you the owner. These you cannot afford to ignore, or then you will be in trouble. You are your own landlord; can you imagine how proud you will be. Oh, yes that is the feeling I am trying to create under your skin.

Once it is there soon or later it is going to break out, and you know what, you are going to be happy about it. Now, let's look at some of the situations you will face in renting. (1) You are helping your landlord out, by paying his mortgage for him, you are saying, he is smarter than you are, so why not look out for him. (2) You are literally putting money in his or her pocket while you are broke. (3) Is it that he is smarter than you, or is that you are not thinking? These are things to think about, because sometimes we find that we just cannot get ahead, but do not stop to analyze our situation.

You will move only when you see it fit to do so. There will not be any Landlord to slip you a notice under the bottom of the door, or in your mail box, to let you know that you have lived here long enough, and it is time to move on. It is possible, the landlord did not like you, but since you were

152

paying his bills, he kept you just for that, now that the apartment needed a face lift, you could go, you were the right person to rent at the time. Now he is showing that he does not need you anymore. It is time to take your bed and walk. You may not like it, but what can you do. You see when this is happening, you know the Landlord controls you and what you do. He decides your movements. This does not have to happen. It was the wise man Solomon that said" A wise man's heart is to the right side, while a foolish man's heart is to the left side". I hope your heart is to your right side. Why not be the wise man. Your Landlord is not telling you what to do, he is doing whatever he wants to do with you. He is in control, so he shows you it's time for you to start thinking on your own. Get your own, put down all the fluffy carpet you can afford, go ahead with your decorations, you are now calling the shot, and then invite your former landlord over. Let him see he is not smarter than you are, it was only a matter of time, before you get it together. If you have the money to purchase for cash, then your situation may be different. Possibility is, were a fortunate winner into the lottery, and that would put you ahead of the game. There is also the possibly of some ancestors that left you some money and you are able to do this without a mortgage, if this is the case, good luck to you. Whatever the case, it is suggest you consult an advisor. When it comes to Real Estate decisions, don't fear the unknown or leave them up to chance! They can help you make the right move, and preventing you from having a night mare. It is possible, with the proper guidance you could make a substantial down payment, hold a mortgage and at the same time be able to use the rest of money to make additional investments. "Very cleaver isn't it" spending time and money on your property will let it value more as the years go by. If you want a deck to do your barbeque, this is the time to make that addition, the home is yours and, whatever is put in to it will be increasing the value, which means more money to you. That is the way the process works until you have completed the improvements you will see your investment coming back to you. More so, when you are ready to sell you will notice a greater difference in the selling process. There is one thing I would like to point out, when you purchase a home and you do the necessary repairs, you are building equity into your property. Some people refer to it as a face lift. Quest what, it worth a lot more than what you have put into it. You can pull some of this money out in the form of equity, and that cash is yours to keep. There could be another purchase or some other investment made with this money, if you are thinking of investing. The money can be taken from the property in the form of refinancing or what is known as an equity line. Some times the amount of money taken out at the time of refinancing would appear that the home is free to you. What I meant is, say you purchase for $100,000 and two years later you take out $125,000, what is the cost of the home to you? For this to happen it has to do with the price paid for the property and what is taken out. Time might have some bearings on all of this. If you are not well versed on what to do, but have a little idea, consult a specialist that is in that field. There might be some intimidation where you are concerned at first, but after a couple of time you will get very comfortable, and be glad you did. Do not let your friends or anyone else intimidate you, or give you negative advise. Remember they will not put money in your pocket, neither will they add dollars to your bank account, so don't listen to them. Negative advices are for discouragement only, once you read this book, I think you will be careful of what to listen to, and the way you do things. I like to listen to some people, and others, I ignore when they are talking. Why? Because some people talking is like an empty barrel rolling, make endless noise with no great significance. What you are getting is something that does not edifies, therefore make no sense.

REAL ESTATE AND PEOPLE

When it comes to Real Estate, everyone has a different reaction. People think differently when it comes to purchasing of a piece of property. If you should ask someone a simple question is, why do you purchase a home? Some people would not have an answer to that simple question. This might sound funny or strange, but if you should ask ten people the same question there would be ten different answers. What I am driving at here is people of different culture and in different parts of the world react differently to real estate. If a simple question should be asked, there would be many different answers, some would say it is a house, some would say it is a plot of land and you never know the other answers that would be given. I heard a young man said once that real estate is a piece of land with the fence around it. As they say different folks, for different strokes. Whatever one might say, investing as a real estate can be a winner, it does not really matter what the culture is, real estate is an investment that should not be taken lightly. I mentioned in previous chapters that buying real estate is one of the biggest transaction one can ever make and should be treated like that. Once we know how to take care of our hard-earned money. We will know how to treat our investment. There are drawbacks with many people when it comes to purchasing real estate. Real Estate is a gold mine, but many of us do not know how to capitalize on it. May be, because we walk on the ground, it does not seem to mean much of a value. This is a precious commodity that we treat and look on lightly but mean the world of good to us. Real Estate is the backbone of an economy, but we have not taken the time to stop, look, and think what this is doing, and can do for us and our families.

REAL ESTATE AND THE COMMUNITY

There is no doubt within my mind that some is going to ask, what does real estate has to do with a community, or what does the community has to do with real estate.? We will agree that real estate is land, and we improve these lands by erecting buildings on them. The next move is to move in the building we live and called that place home. Each person improved on their land and their homes then we called these villages, or we refer to them as our communities.

It does not stop just there, we could make these areas bad communities, or good communities. We determine this by the way we keep our properties, and it would be good if we continue to improve on our properties, or as many like to say, it is my home. You see you determine if you want to make it a home or a house. A house has very little or no feature to it, its condition is not desirable and will let the community look bad and run down if it is not properly maintained. This is not the community that we want to build on. The opposite of this is to build a community that is attractive and desirable. The key to this is to make our real estate our home, and keep our homes in good shape and condition so it beautifies the community. We agree that there will be hard work and plenty to do but it will be worth it after all. Can you imagine, if all home owners in the community take pride in making his or her home the

158

best in the area, what the community would be like? This would attract people from different communities, and villages. On the other hand, what if your neighbor should be selling his or her home, can you imagine what impact your home would be to that property for sale. My word to you is to treat your home as if it will be going on the market the next day. why? Because a well-kept home enhances the community. Periodically a nice coat of painting will make the home look brand new and appealing, which can be done at minimum cost. Many might think of it as very expensive, but with the correct information it is another helpful improvement to your real estate and the community. A well-kept lawn speaks more than a thousand words to those that pass through the community on a whole. People will stop to look at your lawn and make good gesture of it, to top the icing on the cake, with drops of a few lights around your home after painting, and you have finished the lawn. Again, lighting does not have to be expensive. After you have done all this, walk to the front of your home, take a look at it, you might see other little improvements that could be added, like planting a tree or adding a little more decoration to your home. For sure, I could guarantee that the people in the area are going to talk about your home. And not only that, but most of are going to patronize what you have done. A good thing to do after you have finished working on your home, and you think you are satisfied, is to test on the market to see how well you have done. The market will determine your investment. Good luck, and try to be the best at what you do, it will pay off sooner or later.

CAPTION PAGES

The information you have read has been put together by a knowledgeable real estate person, one that love the real estate business and believes highly in it. This is a quite simple article that is easy to be understood, yet a very informative guide that meant to help homebuyers understand the home buying process, and make the right decisions throughout the years to come. The real estate business has thrived and is still thriving today.

The real estate industry is comprised of buying, selling and renting, which will continue as long as this earth remains intact. The idea of buying a home is always the American dream and will continue to be while there is life on this planet. It is the best thing that anyone could think of doing for one self, or love one's retirement, and even your children's education. If you do not think this true, just ask someone that had made their purchase twenty to thirty years ago, and they will confirm it is a fact. Their monthly mortgage payment if any, could be what is being paid today for a studio, or even lower. When we stop today to look at the way rents are high, one could not think otherwise than to purchase their own home. However, while buying a home is important and we encourage home ownership, because it is a wonderful; thing to do. We want you to be well informed, and that is what this book is all about. If you cannot remember to take all the steps mentioned in this book, there is one thing you should remember, "when in doubt seek the advice of an experienced person. Making the wrong decision can cause you hundreds or even thousands of hard- earned dollars, while getting the right person to give the intelligent information could make you thousands of dollars. I want to see you make money on your purchase, but making the wrong and uninformed decision can cost you big before you make any move, gather the information that is relevant to your purchase, whatever you do not understand, ask or go it over until you understand, or ask your friend to go it over with you.

"There is always another thought behind your way of thinking. I cannot forget the phrase that says, two head are better than one" and that bears true today. Someone else will get the answer before you can, or with you.

ACKNOWLEDGEMENTS

It has come to the time to reflect back on the work that I have done, knowing that it was not on my own but as the great writer Paul said in Philippians 4: 13 "I can do all things through Christ that strengthened me". Thanks to my friend that have made such contribution to the success of this book. I will borrow the word of Isaiah when he wrote, "the spirit of the lord was upon me because he hath anointed me to preach the word". The spirit of the Lord was upon me, and I was propelled to write. I was greatly challenged to dig deeply and probe so many crannies to look beyond for situations. This is a testing of my ability, and by doing so, I have documented the results.

It is my wish to express special gratitude to Ms. L loy Cuthbert who have worked with so diligently. You have shown remarkable sensitivity and depth of knowledge. To Ms. Kegrah Whittingham, I thank you for the encouragement, you have taken the time helping me with my typing. Your dedication will not be forgotten. Ms. Sharon Watson you will not be forgotten your encouraging word will always be ringing in my ears. Christine McPherson told me that you believe in me, and that I well, so, here it is, you may read all about it! To Ms. Carol Francis, what would I have done without you? You have shown diligence in your skills and all that seem impossible, you have made them possible. You have shown remarkable sensitivity and depth of knowledge. To me you are like the carpenter's plane. He uses the plane to make the rough edges of the wood smooth, and from that he turned out pieces of the nicest furniture. I applaud you, Carol. To Mr. Gary Reid, you have done a tremendous job. In addition, I wish to acknowledge the countless individuals, organizations that so generously offered ideas information, reviewed copies of this book. The information contained in this book grew out of my past experiences. Sincerest thanks to all who have helped to paved the way for this to have happened. Finally, to God be the glory who has given me knowledge wisdom and understanding. I am still standing as the wise man Solomon, asking for more wisdom.

This book is written with great concern for those people that want to get into real estate and do not know how or where to start. As a realtor with years of experience, I have compiled a wealth of knowledge to help buyers and sellers alike. I have worked as a vocational Instructor teaching young people carpentry and cabinet, so they can get and keep a job. I have also a real estate broker and instructor, I have helped many potential buyers became happy homeowners. In this book you are motivated to be what you wanted to be! I have shared my experience how I started as an investor.

As a mortgage broker, I have explained the use of credit card and the best way of utilizing them so as to not slave for your card each month. I took in account sellers that want to market their properties, and are in need of help. The mind is a powerful thing and should not be waisted. My philosophy is, teach a person to fish and feed him for life instead of feeding him for the day. The writer has explained to the buyer how he or she can calculate their monthly mortgage payment. There you will see the parties that are involve in the real estate buying and selling process, even what happen at the closing when buyer takes position of the property.

Thaddeus Faulknor is a native of Jamaica's West Indies. He has traveled to many different islands and countries, including Bermuda, where he worked on the South Hampton Princess Hotel as a finish carpenter. He later taught vocational education in Jamaica. His hopes were to one day write a book to share his experience. Mr. Faulknor migrated to the United States in 1979, and took up residency in Yonkers, New York. There, he continued in the woodworking trade while pursuing his education in business administration and later became a real estate broker. He has never ceased to strive to become better. His hard work and family dedication has led him to obtain two United States patents. His testimony is, "You can make it if you try" and "Thank God for his marvelous grace towards me."

www.ingramcontent.com/pod-product-compliance
Lightning Source LLC
Chambersburg PA
CBHW040855210326
41597CB00029B/4859